The Hong Kong Economic Policy Studies Series

LABOUR MARKET
IN A DYNAMIC ECONOMY

LABOUR MARKET
IN A DYNAMIC ECONOMY

Wing Suen
William Chan

Published for

The Hong Kong Centre for Economic Research
The Hong Kong Economic Policy Studies Forum

by

City University of Hong Kong Press

First published 1997
Printed in Hong Kong

ISBN 962-937-012-3

Published by
City University of Hong Kong Press
City University of Hong Kong
Tat Chee Avenue, Kowloon, Hong Kong

Internet: http://www.cityu.edu.hk/upress/
E-mail: upress@cityu.edu.hk

The free-style calligraphy on the cover, *lao,* means "labour" in Chinese.

Contents

Detailed Chapter Contents

Foreword

The key to the economic success of Hong Kong has been a business and policy environment which is simple, predictable and transparent. Experience shows that prosperity results from policies that protect private property rights, maintain open and competitive markets, and limit the role of the government.

The rapid structural change of Hong Kong's economy in recent years has generated considerable debate over the proper role of economic policy in the future. The restoration of sovereignty over Hong Kong from Britain to China has further complicated the debate. Anxiety persists as to whether the pre-1997 business and policy environment of Hong Kong will continue.

During this period of economic and political transition in Hong Kong, various interested parties will be re-assessing Hong Kong's existing economic policies. Inevitably, they will advocate an agenda aimed at altering the present policy making framework to reshape the future course of public policy.

For this reason, it is of paramount importance for those familiar with economic affairs to reiterate the reasons behind the success of the economic system in the past, to identify what the challenges are for the future, to analyze and understand the economy sector by sector, and to develop appropriate policy solutions to achieve continued prosperity.

In a conversation with my colleague Y. F. Luk, we came upon the idea of inviting economists from universities in Hong Kong to take up the challenge of examining systematically the economic policy issues of Hong Kong. An expanding group of economists (The Hong Kong Economic Policy Studies Forum) met several times to give form and shape to our initial ideas. The Hong Kong Economic Policy Studies Project was then launched in 1996 with some 30 economists from the universities in Hong Kong and a few from overseas. This is the first time in Hong Kong history that a concerted public effort has been undertaken by academic economists in the territory. It represents a joint expression of our collective concerns, our hopes for a better Hong Kong, and our faith in the economic future.

The Hong Kong Centre for Economic Research is privileged to be co-ordinating this Project. The unfailing support of many distinguished citizens in our endeavour and their words of encouragement are especially gratifying. We also thank the directors and editors of the City University of Hong Kong Press and The Commercial Press (H.K.) Ltd. for their enthusiasm and dedication which extends far beyond the call of duty.

Yue-Chim Richard Wong
Director
The Hong Kong Centre
for Economic Research

Foreword by the Series Editor

It is well known that Hong Kong is not rich in natural resources other than having a deep-water harbour. The extraordinary achievements of the Hong Kong economy in the past few decades are to a great extent due to its productive and good quality human resources.

Human resources are very heterogeneous in background. The three million people in the labour force differ vastly in terms of their knowledge, skills, job preferences and aspirations. The positions offered by firms and industries also differ widely regarding job duties, compensations, work environments and career paths. It is obvious that mismatch of workers and jobs can be quite detrimental to the economic well being of society. In a free market economy, a major function of the labour market is to allocate human resources efficiently through the "invisible hand".

The labour market is also instrumental in directly or indirectly encouraging investment in human capital and enhancing the quality of human resources. These include on-the-job training, the acquisition of work experience, and the provision of incentives for further schooling and education. The outstanding performance of the Hong Kong economy is clear evidence that its labour market has been functioning well.

It is remarkable that the labour market has weathered many drastic shocks and extensive changes in the past decades, including massive immigration and emigration, rapid population growth, mass education, rising female participation, labour import, labour legislation, business cycles and structural transformation. It is quite fortunate that the labour market has been flexible enough and adjusting effectively so that it has contributed to Hong Kong's impressive economic growth despite all these disturbances.

How has the Hong Kong labour market developed over these turbulent years? How has it successfully dealt with the above challenges? What are the likely difficulties and important issues in the foreseeable future? What appropriate policies should be adopted by the government? These are the main questions addressed in this book.

The authors of this book, Dr. Wing Suen and Dr. William Chan, are both long time researchers in the field of labour economics. Using census and survey data, they have also carried out empirical research on various aspects of the labour market. Their discussion and analysis of the Hong Kong labour market in the dynamic economy of Hong Kong are of high standards and authoritative.

The authors investigate in detail the impacts on the labour market of female participation, immigration, and sectoral shifts. Each of these separate investigations indicates that the market has functioned efficiently. They also discuss issues that have lately been publicly debated, including labour retraining, labour import, immigration, and employment legislation.

The labour market has important implications to the well being of every individual employer and employee, as well as to the economy as a whole. As Hong Kong enters a new stage as a Special Administrative Region of China, the developments and policies on the labour market are naturally of great public concern. This book should become a standard reference on the subject.

Y. F. Luk
School of Economics and Finance
The University of Hong Kong

Preface

We would like to thank two anonymous referees for their helpful comments. We would also like to thank Roger Yip and Linda Yung for their assistance in our research for this book, and to Florence Yip Wai Man, Chung Choi Chu and Liu Shing Wah for preparing the Chinese translation.

Wing Suen
Senior Lecturer
School of Economics and Finance
The University of Hong Kong

William Chan
Lecturer
School of Economics and Finance
The University of Hong Kong

List of Illustrations

Figures

Tables

CHAPTER 1

Introduction

Adam Smith opened his inquiry of *The Wealth of Nations* with a discussion on division of labour. His detailed depiction of a pin factory makes us all aware of the enormous productivity gains that can be reaped from specialization. Today economists are again focusing on labour, particularly skills embodied in human capital, as the source of economic growth. It is not an exaggeration to claim that a well functioning labour market is the key to economic success. The two major functions of a successful labour market are to co-ordinate the division of labour and to encourage the accumulation of human capital.

The benefits from specialization are significant, but the problems it brings are daunting. Economic growth is associated with the provision of new goods and services as well as with new ways of doing things. For example, a few years ago no one dreamed that "Web-page" designers would soon exist in large numbers. How does society prepare people for the increasingly specialized skills needed to perform the infinite variety of tasks in a modern economy? Economic growth is associated with a ruthless abandonment of things that have lost their competitive advantage. The rickshaw coolie in Hong Kong, for example, is a vestige of the past. Ivory carving used to be a highly skilled craft that required years of training; an international treaty has virtually wiped out this trade overnight. How does the economy accommodate the constant flow of people whose specialized skills become obsolete?

In broader terms, the problems of labour shortage and unemployment are also the result of division of labour. If everyone were to become self-sufficient, there would be neither an excess demand for nor an excess supply of labour. But the society would of course be vastly poorer, too.

As a dynamic economy in a fast-growing region, Hong Kong has seen its fair share of the benefits and the problems arising from the differentiation of its labour force. The openness of Hong Kong's economy enables it to take maximum advantage of the international division of labour. Hong Kong is now one of the world's major exporters and an international centre for doing business. Although the transformation of the economy has brought wealth to the people, this has come with growing pains. Hong Kong has over several decades witnessed waves of immigration and emigration. Large and erratic shifts in labour supply have created opportunities but have put strains on the economy. How the labour market adapts to these challenges is the theme of this book.

Hong Kong has one of the most flexible labour markets in the world. This makes the city's experience worth recounting. Understanding how Hong Kong's labour market adapts to the changing environment will help one to appreciate the market mechanism at work. Public policy options of labour strategies for Hong Kong considered in this book are based on our guiding principle that market forces rather than government interventions should primarily be relied upon.

Outline of the Book

A book of this length cannot provide a comprehensive treatment of the labour market in Hong Kong. We try to be selective by focusing only on the developments over the past thirty or so years. A detailed study of the condition of human resources during the early stage of Hong Kong's industrial take-off would be extremely interesting, but records are too sketchy to allow us to perform a study of that period.

Chapter 2 presents a brief history of the Hong Kong labour market since 1961. It covers topics such as fluctuations in the size of the population, changes in the pattern of labour force participation, and growth in labour earnings. Labour is not a homogeneous factor of production, and the composition of the workforce matters just as much as the total quantity of workers. The chapter discusses some salient features of the changing composition of the working population, including the improvement in educational attainment, the rising influence of female workers, and the changing mix of industry and occupation. Although the labour market in Hong Kong is highly competitive, it does not function according to textbook models of perfect competition. Near the end of Chapter 2 we provide a short summary of the major institutional developments that have shaped the operation of the labour market.

Our account of the history of the labour market relies heavily on quantitative evidence. Developments in the labour market are complex and often imperceptible; it is only when changes are measured quantitatively that they become evident. For example, a person caught in the middle of the structural transformation of the Hong Kong economy may be more aware of the costs than of the benefits of structural change. With hindsight — and when measured with numbers — the benefits would become crystal clear. As another example, selective personal experience may lead one to conclude that immigrants are taking jobs away from local workers. When measured carefully, however, the statistical evidence for this conclusion is extremely skimpy.

In Chapter 3 we take a detailed look at three major developments in the labour market of Hong Kong. This chapter owes a lot to recent econometric research that makes use of census records released by the Census and Statistics Department. By looking at the actual effects of specific episodes of labour market change, we go beyond verbal arguments about the competitiveness of the labour market to gain a better understanding of the market in action.

In particular, Chapter 3 analyzes the effects of the entry of women into the labour force, the effects of immigration on local workers, and the effects of structural shifts in the economy. These three different areas of research all indicate that the Hong Kong labour market is highly flexible in the face of large shocks in labour demand or supply. Such shocks illustrate the important role of economic incentives and of the self-adjusting price mechanism in the labour market.

In spite of its success, the labour market is not free of flaws. In Chapter 4 we identify several major challenges facing the labour market at this juncture of political and economic transition. The decline of manufacturing industries, the globalization of the economy, and the evolving political structure all pose potential problems that would affect the labour market.

There is evidence that wage inequality is on the rise. Large numbers of displaced workers have withdrawn from the labour force, and long-term unemployment is creeping up. How to ensure that less-skilled workers will continue to, contribute to and to share in the gains from, economic growth is and will be a major task facing the society of Hong Kong. At the other end of the skills spectrum, demand for skilled and professional workers is growing as the Hong Kong economy transforms itself into an international centre of commerce and finance. Some sectors in the economy are facing labour shortages. Many employees today are realizing that their existing human resources do not possess the requisite skills to suit the new demands.

Labour market mismatch at the micro level is compounded by a pronounced trend towards internationalization of the Hong Kong labour force. Waves of emigration and return migration have produced a large pool of people who can return to Hong Kong with valuable international experience. However, the same people can leave Hong Kong at short notice too. Immigration from China will also become a more pressing issue now that the change of sovereignty has completed. Meanwhile, business and unions continue to closely scrutinize imported workers at all skill levels. Balancing the claims of diverse interests will require economic judgement as well as political wisdom on the part of policy makers.

The degree to which the labour market will remain flexible will depend on the nature and extent of political intervention. In the second half of Chapter 4 we discuss the role of the political process in shaping policies concerning labour importation, employee retraining, and manpower planning.

The challenges identified in Chapter 4 provide the basis for evaluating policy options for the labour market. Such options are explored in Chapter 5. We divide these policy options into two broad groups: those dealing with demand-supply mismatch and those relating to labour market institutions.

The government's response to demand-supply mismatch includes the introduction of labour importation schemes and employee retraining programmes. We argue that employee retraining programmes should focus primarily on providing short-term help with getting displaced workers back to work, rather than on intensive government-sponsored training courses. The government should also assist firms to conduct on-the-job training because it is usually more effective. With some qualifications, we do not support the importation of low-skilled workers. Labour importation tends to damage industrial relations without providing a long-term solution to the problem of labour shortage. A long-term plan for human resources should centre around education and immigration policies.

The politicization of the policy-making process has generated many new proposals for reforming labour market institutions. Chapter 5 evaluates a few of these proposals, including equal opportunity, unfair dismissal, and job security policies. Our evaluation is formed on the basis of economic theory and the experience of other countries that have tried similar policies. However, many relevant pieces of data are not available in Hong Kong. We recommend that the government be more willing to release data for academic and policy evaluation purposes. Finally, we hope that this volume itself will demonstrate how a modest amount of data can profitably be used to inform public policy in Hong Kong.

CHAPTER 2

A Quantitative History of the Labour Market

In 1961 the Hong Kong economy was poised for an industrial take-off. The industrialization process was fuelled by a large supply of relatively unskilled but hardworking labour, many of whom were refugees from China. Today Hong Kong is on the cusp of another political and economic transition. The dominance of manufacturing has been largely displaced by commerce and the service sector, and the demand for unskilled labour is falling relative to the demand for skilled and educated workers. Immigration remains a perennial issue, but people's attitude towards immigrant workers are changing. Although the problems that concern us now are quite different from those that faced us some thirty years ago, the labour market has always been a crucial component in the economic development of Hong Kong. And it will remain so in the future, for Hong Kong is but a barren rock built on human capital.

We begin our brief history of the Hong Kong labour market with the year 1961, when the government launched its first post-war census of the population. Information about labour market conditions prior to this time is sketchy and unreliable.

A twenty-year-old worker enumerated in the 1961 census would be near retirement age today. If we were to follow his labour-market history, perhaps the most remarkable change would be the increase in his wage earnings over time. In 1961 the average daily wage for a semi-skilled worker was less than HK$7 (Riedel 1974). In 1995 craftsmen and operatives in manufacturing industries earned an average wage of HK$280 a day (Census and Statistics

Department 1996). Correcting for changes in the value of the dollar, this still represents a more than four-fold increase in real wages. This calculation ignores life cycle effects, but the long term improvement in real earnings is unmistakable.

It is highly improbable that we would find a worker who stayed with the same employer from 1961 through the ensuing period under our study. Occupations such as bus conductors or ivory workers no longer exist, and industries such as wig factories are hardly hiring any more. In the United States a typical individual holds more than ten jobs at different stages of his working life. In a rapidly developing economy like Hong Kong, labour market transitions must be much more frequent. As old jobs disappear, new opportunities constantly arise. The financial sector has greatly expanded its employment opportunities, and innovations in telecommunications have given rise to many new occupations. Paging companies and Internet service providers were unheard of in the 1960s. Due to changing economic and personal circumstances, labour market transitions are inevitable. Some of these transitions would be voluntary quits, and they would usually bring about increases in wage earnings. In other instances a worker might have lost his job because the company he was working for closed down or laid off its employees. Such changes would cause temporary setbacks and difficulties. A worker caught in the middle of this process may not appreciate this, but with hindsight one thing is clear: on the whole, the new jobs are more productive than are the ones they displace. The labour market transition process, painful as it may be at times, is an inherent part of the long-run growth in labour earnings.

A perceptive worker would also witness many gradual changes in his work environment. He would find that an increasing number of his co-workers were female, and some of them might have risen above his level. At different times, he would feel threatened by the influx of refugee workers willing to work at low wages. As time passes, however, he would not be able to tell the immigrant workers apart from the locals. The worker would also find that young new entrants to the labour force were becoming better educated and that more and more jobs had formal educational requirements. These and other changes in the labour market are the subject of this chapter.

Growth of the Labour Force

According to the 1961 population census, the size of the economically active population was approximately 1.2 million during that year. The economically active population, or the labour force, consists of people engaged in gainful employment or actively seeking work. The labour force had grown to 3.1 million by 1996. Such long-term increases in the size of the labour force would not deserve comment were it not for one common misconception about the labour market, which we call here the "fallacy of scarce jobs".

The fallacy of scarce jobs, sometimes also called the "lump of labour fallacy" (see *The Economist*, 25 November 1995), wrongly maintains that the number of tasks to be fulfilled in an economy is limited or even fixed. According to this logic, immigrants will take jobs away from natives, and women who enter the labour force will displace men from their work. This fallacy is also responsible for the common practice of measuring the economic gains from a project or policy by the number of jobs it creates. John Maynard Keynes (1964) once remarked that to dig holes in the ground will generate new employment and will increase the national dividend. The second part of his remark is surely wrong. Jobs — unlike commodities — are not scarce. In fact, scarcity implies that the number of jobs is unlimited. Human desires being insatiable, people will want more computers, better cars, new books for spiritual nourishment, and so on, *ad infinitum*. More goods are desired than can ever be produced. It follows that there are too many, not too few, jobs. The economic problem is not to increase the number of jobs but to allocate scarce resources to those tasks that are valued most.

The historical experience of Hong Kong and of other countries flatly rejects the scarce jobs fallacy. If the number of jobs were truly fixed, the 1.2 million jobs available in 1961 could not

Figure 2.1
Size of the Hong Kong Labour Force, 1961–96

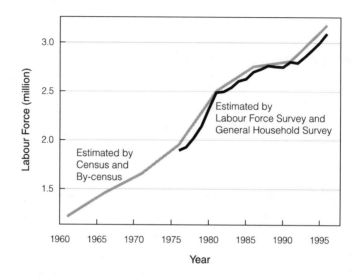

Source: Hong Kong Census and Statistics Department (various years).

accommodate the 1.9 million people who have been added to the
labour force in the past 35 years, and the current unemployment
rate would be over 60%! Such a conclusion is absurd. Hong Kong
has managed to maintain more or less full employment amid rapid
growth in its economically active population. The notion that the
number of jobs is fixed must be expunged.

The growth of the Hong Kong labour force has not been
smooth and steady. Figure 2.1 plots the size of the labour force in
various years. The dotted line is based on data from censuses and
by-censuses conducted every five years. The solid line shows annual
labour force figures from the Labour Force Surveys and the
subsequent General Household Surveys.

A close look at Figure 2.1 reveals three distinct periods of
labour force growth:

  1. 1961–81: During this period the size of the labour force
     grew from 1.2 million to 2.5 million. The annual rate of

increase was 3.7%. The influx of refugees from China accounted for a large part of the increase. Rising female labour force participation was another factor behind the growth of the labour force. It is fortunate that the labour supply increased so rapidly, as labour-intensive industries were still the mainstay of the Hong Kong economy in that period.

2. 1981–92: In 1980 the government abolished the "touch base" policy, which allowed refugees to stay in Hong Kong once they had reached its urban areas. Since then legal and illegal immigration has continued, but at a much reduced rate. The growth of the labour force decelerated as a result. Following the signing of the Joint Declarations in 1984, it was agreed that China would resume sovereignty over Hong Kong in 1997. Political uncertainty over the future of Hong Kong induced a large wave of emigration that further depleted the stock of the working population. As a result, the size of the labour force increased only at a modest rate of 1.1% a year. In the latter part of this period Hong Kong experienced a labour shortage in its fast-expanding service sector.

3. 1992–96: Emigrants from Hong Kong met an economic slowdown in Canada, the United States, Australia, and other countries. Meanwhile, fuelled by a reinvigorated Chinese economy, growth in Hong Kong remained strong. For economic and personal reasons, many Hong Kong people returned after they obtained a foreign passport. One of the authors (Suen 1995a) estimates that the balance between emigration and return migration turned from a net outflow of 41,000 people in 1990–92 to a net inflow of 82,000 people in 1992–94. Largely because of this flow of return immigrants, labour force growth revived to an annual rate of 2.6%. In merely four years the size of the labour force increased from 2.8 million to 3.1 million.

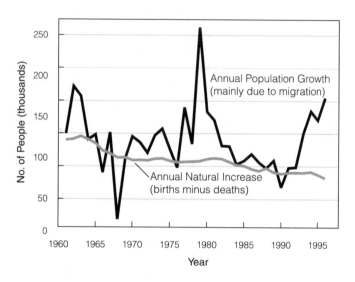

Figure 2.2
Annual Changes in the Population, 1961–96

Source: Hong Kong Census and Statistics Department (various years).

Shifts in the Demographic Structure

Changes in the size of the labour force can be attributed to two factors: changes in the population base and changes in the pattern of labour force participation. The population in Hong Kong doubled from 3.1 million in 1961 to 6.3 million in 1996. Part of this population growth is due to natural increase (i.e., the excess of births over deaths). Fluctuations in the flow of immigration and emigration constitute another major part of the change in the overall population level.

Figure 2.2 plots the annual changes in the size of the Hong Kong population (solid line). With the exception of the year 1968, population growth has been positive. However, the rate of increase has been quite irregular. It ranged from an annual growth of 5.6% in 1979 to an annual growth of only 0.3% in 1990. One of the challenges for the labour market is to adapt quickly to such large swings in the population base.

While overall population growth has been volatile, Figure 2.2 also shows that the natural increase in population has been following a steady decline (dotted line). The rate of natural increase fell dramatically from twenty-eight per thousand in 1961 to five per thousand in 1996 — less than one-fifth of its previous level. The fall in the death rate has not kept pace with the even more rapid fall in births. Rising income and the increasing costs of child care, both in terms of the time cost of women and the cost of housing space, have contributed to the secular decline in fertility. Table 2.1 shows that the total fertility rate (i.e., the total number of live births per woman during her reproductive life if the age-specific birth rates of a year are fixed) was higher in Hong Kong than in other developed countries in 1970. Fertility has declined worldwide since then, but the decline was especially pronounced for Hong Kong. The total fertility rate in Hong Kong is now the lowest in the world.

A total fertility rate of 1.2 children per woman is not sufficient to keep the population growing in the long run. In fact the size of the population aged below thirty shrunk from 2.9 million in 1986 to 2.6 million in 1996. Improved life expectancy and reduced fertility also tend to produce an aging population. In 1996 there were on average 7.1 people aged between 15 and 64 to support each person aged over 65. This ratio is projected to fall to six to one by the year 2011 (Census and Statistics Department 1992a). Barring increased immigration, the Hong Kong labour market will eventually have to cope with a shrinking population base and an aging demographic structure.

Natural increase, however, is not the only source of population growth. As shown in Figure 2.2 above, there is a sizable gap between the overall change in population and the change due to natural increase. The difference is attributable to a net in-migration of people into the territory. In the period 1961–96 more than a third of the overall population growth was due to net population inflows.

Since fertility and mortality patterns change slowly, fluctuations in population growth are mainly due to fluctuations in migration. Hong Kong has experienced several waves of immigration and emigration during the period under study. In the early

Table 2.1
Total Fertility Rates in Selected Countries, 1970 and 1993

	1970	1993
Canada	2.2	1.9
China	5.8	2.0
France	2.4	1.7
Germany	1.9	1.3
Hong Kong	**3.3**	**1.2**
India	5.5	3.7
Japan	2.0	1.5
Korea, Republic of	4.3	1.7
Singapore	3.0	1.7
Sweden	2.0	2.1
United Kingdom	2.2	1.8
United States	2.2	2.1
World Average	4.8	3.2

Source:　The World Bank (1995). *World Development Report 1995*, Oxford: Oxford University Press.

Note:　Figures refer to the average number of live births per woman according to age-specific birth rates of that year.

1960s failure of the Great Leap Forward in China resulted in a massive outflow of refugees trying to escape famine. Riots and social instability in Hong Kong around 1967 interrupted the net inflow as many local residents emigrated to foreign countries. The immigrant wave from China then gradually built up again in the late 1970s, thanks to a more relaxed political climate in China and to loosened border control. In 1979 net immigration reached the height of 200,000 people, and the Hong Kong government began to take measures to restrict the inflow from China. Border control was strengthened. Government policy changed in 1980 such that illegal immigrants from China were immediately repatriated once they were caught. Employers are now required to check the resident status of all job seekers. Largely because of these measures the wave of immigration subsided in the 1980s.

Beginning in the second half of the 1980s more and more Hong Kong people began leaving the territory in anticipation of the change of sovereignty. The bloody suppression of student demonstrations in Beijing in 1989 speeded up the exodus. In 1990 the balance between immigration and emigration showed a net outflow of some 20,000 people. The nature of this wave of emigration, however, was quite different from that of the one that occurred around 1967. Economic conditions in Hong Kong are now comparable to those of the host countries admitting Hong Kong emigrants. Many of those who left only wanted to obtain a foreign passport for "insurance" purposes and had no firm intention of permanently staying in the host countries. Once they had satisfied the residence requirements many returned, resulting in a minor population boom in the past few years.

The flow of return immigrants coincides with a number of developments that merit attention. First, as Hong Kong gains an international reputation as an economic powerhouse, more and more foreigners come to work in the city. The number of work visas issued to "professionals and persons with technical, administrative or managerial skills" rose from 13,900 in 1992 to 18,800 in 1994. The number of Britons (who did not need work visas) staying in Hong Kong went up from 18,400 to 23,800 during the same period, even though the British government recently retreated from its colony. Second, economic integration with China has accelerated since the late 1980s. A survey in 1995 showed 122,000 Hong Kong residents working in China, up 90% from a similar survey taken just three years before (Census and Statistics Department 1997). The number of Chinese workers employed by Hong Kong businesspeople in China is widely believed to exceed the size of the total labour force in Hong Kong. Informal estimates by the Hong Kong press of the size of this labour pool range from four to six million. These two developments, coupled with the potential inflow and outflow of the many people with residence rights both in Hong Kong and in overseas countries, mean that the Hong Kong labour market cannot be considered in isolation from the world economic system.

Labour Force Participation

Even if the population base were to remain stable, people's labour force participation decisions would still change the size of the labour force. In 1996 the labour force participation rate was 61.8%. The remaining 38.2% of the population were economically inactive. These include, among others, students, home-makers, and retirees. Understanding the factors behind labour participation decisions is an important component of understanding long-term changes in labour supply.

When discussing labour supply it is important to distinguish between the supply of labour to a particular firm or industry and the supply of labour to the economy. The supply of labour to a particular firm or industry can be highly responsive to wages as workers seek the most profitable employment. The supply of labour to the economy, on the other hand, is typically less elastic because the next best alternative — namely, leisure — need not be particularly attractive. Pencavel (1986) summarizes a large body of empirical research in the United States and Britain showing that the labour supply of prime age men is rather unresponsive to changes in wages. The experience in Hong Kong confirms this result.

Figure 2.3 plots the age-specific labour force participation rates of men for the years 1966, 1981, and 1995. Labour force participation among those aged 25 to 44 was close to 100% and hardly changed over the years during which the level of wages improved dramatically. For the 15 to 24 age group, the male labour force participation rate declined from 66% in 1966 to 51% in 1995. This was mainly due to improvements in education opportunities. Figure 2.3 also shows that there was a marked drop in the labour participation of older men. As a result of rising income, leisure becomes more valuable and people retire earlier. Suen (1997) estimates that the average retirement age for men in Hong Kong fell from 67.8 years in 1976 to 66.3 years in 1991.

In the young (15–24) and old (55 and above) age groups, changes in female labour participation were broadly similar to those for men. Figure 2.4 shows that labour participation dropped among younger women, primarily because women too were getting more schooling. Rising affluence also meant that elderly women could reduce their labour participation.

Whereas labour force participation for prime age men has remained stable, Figure 2.4 shows a notable increase in the labour supply of prime age women. For example, the labour force participation rate among 25- to 29-year old women rose from 38% in 1966 to 83% in 1995. Several factors can account for this big rise in female labour participation. First, Hong Kong women have been marrying at a later age. The median age at first marriage for women increased from 22.9 years in 1971 to 26.3 years in 1990 (Census and Statistics Department 1992b). Since single females are more likely to participate in market work than married women, deferred marriage would tend to increase labour participation. Second, fertility has been falling in Hong Kong. Reduced childcare responsibilities again promote labour participation. To be sure, deferred marriage and reduced fertility can be the result, as well as the cause, of higher female labour participation rates. During the period under study, there were marked improvements in education and work opportunities for women. Social attitudes have also become more sympathetic towards career women. However, even in 1995 the female labour force participation rate for the 35- to 54-year-old age group was only slightly over 50%. The comparable figure for the United States was above 70%. There is probably still room for further increases in female labour force participation in Hong Kong.

Employment Status and Unemployment

People in the labour force can be divided into two groups: the working population (those who currently have a job) and the unemployed (those who are actively looking for work). The government of Hong Kong did not collect regular unemployment

Chapter 2

Figure 2.3
Male Age-Specific Labour Participation Rates, Hong Kong 1966, 1981,1995

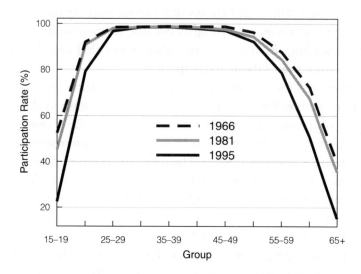

Source: Hong Kong Census and Statistics Department (various years).

Figure 2.4
Female Age-Specific Labour Participation Rates, Hong Kong 1966, 1981,1995

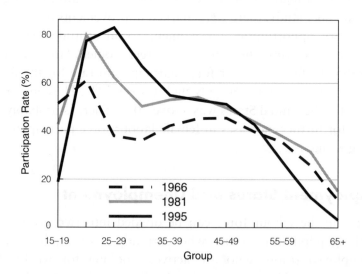

Source: Hong Kong Census and Statistics Department (various years).

Table 2.2
Activity Status of the Working Population, 1961–96
(%)

	1961	1971	1981	1991	1996
Employee	80.4	86.9	88.6	87.8	88.2
Self-employed	10.4	8.3	6.1	5.4	4.2
Employer	4.8	2.6	3.7	5.6	6.7
Unpaid worker	4.4	2.2	1.6	1.2	0.9

Source: Various issues of census and by-census reports.

Note: Figures are based on various census reports. "Employees" include outworkers and student workers.

statistics until 1976. A year before that Hong Kong experienced the most severe "recession" in its post-war history (with a real GDP growth of 0.3%). The Census and Statistics Department began a preliminary Labour Force Survey in September 1975 and recorded an unemployment rate of 9.1%. It was a difficult year for Hong Kong workers. Fortunately, the unemployment rate quickly came down in the following year and never came near 9.1% again for the next twenty years. Figure 2.5 shows the evolution of the unemployment rate in Hong Kong. The mean unemployment rate in the 1976–96 period was 2.9%, and unemployment stayed below 4% in 18 of these 21 years.

The distribution of activity status among the employed population is displayed in Table 2.2. The table shows that the proportion of the working population who are unpaid workers (usually working in small family businesses) or self-employed has fallen steadily over time. The reduction in the population of the self-employed is mainly accounted for by the diminishing role of street hawking. With the shrinking size of the informal sector, the formal wage employment relationship has grown in importance. When Turner (1980) described employment relationships in Hong Kong in the 1970s, he made a distinction between permanent employees, long-term casual workers, and short-term casual workers. The distinction reflected different degrees of job security,

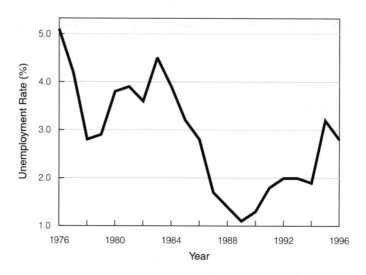

Figure 2.5
Unemployment Rates in Hong Kong, 1976–96

Source: Hong Kong Census and Statistics Department (various years).

of which short-term casual workers had none. Such a distinction has largely disappeared. Today, any employee who works continuously for the same employer for four weeks or more for at least 18 hours in each of the four weeks is regarded as working under a "continuous contract", and the employment relationship is subject to the provisions of the Employment Ordinance. The role of the Employment Ordinance will be discussed in greater detail in the final section of this chapter.

As in any other labour market, workers' employment conditions differ widely across employers. Employees of large companies, of public utilities, and of the government typically enjoy more fringe benefits and have greater job security than employees of small firms. This has led some analysts to make a distinction between the "primary sector" and the "secondary sector". However, the line between these two sectors is not sharply drawn, and worker mobility across it is not uncommon. In recent years deregulation, downsizing, and competitive pressures have caused many large companies to change their employment practices, thereby blurring the distinction even more between these two segments of the labour market.

An interesting phenomenon in Hong Kong's history of employment relationships is the rise and fall of "outwork". Outworkers are individuals who take their work home and are not limited to being physically in the firm. It is a particularly flexible form of employment. Outworkers can avoid the costs of commuting and they can set their own pace at work. For firms, outwork is similar to subcontracting and is particularly suited to small batch manufacturing concerns facing fluctuating demand.

In the 1960s outworkers accounted for less than 1% of the working population in Hong Kong. Starting in the 1970s outwork became an increasingly popular form of wage employment. In 1976, 3.6% of the working population were outworkers. Among women in the 35–54 age group this fraction was 19% (Wong 1983; Tai-Lok Lui 1994). According to research conducted by Richard Wong, the mid-1970s was a period with an unusually large number of young women at childbearing age, and outworking was a particularly attractive form of employment for women with young children in relatively low-income families. Since the 1980s, this cohort of women has found outworking less attractive as their children have grown and their families have become more prosperous. The availability of a massive supply of cheap labour in China also lured manufacturers away from subcontracting their work to outworkers. The proportion of outworkers in the working population fell to 2.4% in 1981 and further to 1.8% in 1986. In 1991 outworkers ceased to exist as a separate category in the official classification of employment status.

Changes in the Composition of the Labour Force

Labour is not a homogeneous commodity, and the labour market is actually a set of inter-related markets for various type of labour services. One of the most important functions of the labour market is to allocate different talents to work on different tasks. Changes in

Chapter 2

Figure 2.6
Female Labour Force Participation Rates, Hong Kong and Other Countries

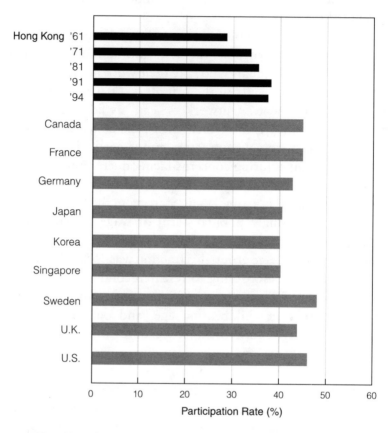

Source: Hong Kong Census and Statistics Department (various years); International
          Labour Office (various years).

Note: Statistics for countries other than Hong Kong are for 1994.

the composition of labour would therefore necessitate adjustments
in the labour market even in the absence of changes in the overall
size of the labour force.

Perhaps the most obvious change in labour composition is the
increase in the proportion of female workers. Figure 2.6 shows a
steady rise in the percentage of women in the labour force from
1961 to 1991. This percentage, however, has not increased in the
past few years. Figure 2.6 also shows that female labour

Table 2.3
Changing Age Structure of the Labour Force, 1961–96
(%)

Age group	1961	1971	1981	1991	1996
under 15	2.0	2.1	–	–	–
15–24	19.1	30.1	30.0	17.5	14.5
25–34	29.1	17.7	27.9	34.6	31.8
35–44	25.2	21.2	15.2	24.6	28.6
45–54	16.7	17.2	15.1	12.7	15.9
55–64	6.4	9.3	8.8	8.2	7.3
65 and over	1.5	2.3	3.0	2.4	1.9
Median age (years)	34.9	35.0	31.8	34.4	36.0

Source: Various issues of census reports.

Note: – means negligible.

participation in Hong Kong still lags behind that of many other countries. In 1994, 37% of the workforce in Hong Kong were female. The comparable figures for Singapore, the United States, and Sweden are 40%, 46%, and 48%, respectively (International Labour Office 1995).

The overall increase in the fraction of women in the workforce is less significant than the fact that women are breaking into many occupations hitherto dominated by men. While there are still more male lawyers than female lawyers, the number of female law students is now greater than that of male law students. Women can now be seen working as taxi drivers and bus drivers, which would have been a rare sight thirty years ago. Occupational segregation still exists in varying degrees, but the barriers are much more permeable nowadays.

Table 2.3 shows changes in the age structure of the labour force. Since immigrants are on average younger than the native population, the large wave of immigration during the 1970s produced a sharp decline in the median age of the workforce. After 1981 immigration from China subsided, and the median age of the workforce rose again, reaching 36 in 1996. Although the median age of the labour force has increased in recent years, the proportion

Chapter 2

Table 2.4
Labour Force by Place of Birth and by Years of Residence, 1976–91
(%)

	1976	1981	1986	1991
Place of birth				
Hong Kong	44.3	45.9	53.4	57.0
China, Taiwan, and Macau	52.6	50.3	42.2	37.0
Elsewhere	3.1	3.8	4.3	6.0
Duration of residence				
5 years or less	n.a.	10.1	n.a.	6.0
Over 5 years	n.a.	89.9	n.a.	94.0

Note: All figures are in percentage terms. Tabulations are based on unpublished
         census files; n.a. means not available.

of older workers (aged 55 or above) has fallen. Declining labour
participation among the elderly has more than offset the growth in
the elderly population. Table 2.3 also shows that the proportion of
young workers (aged 15 to 24) has fallen substantially since 1971.
As a result, the labour force in Hong Kong has shown a greater
concentration of prime-age workers.

In Table 2.4 the composition of the workforce by place of birth
is displayed. As a relatively young city, only 57% of the Hong Kong
workforce are native born. The proportion of workers born in
China fell over the years but remained at a substantial 37% in 1991.
Because a significant proportion of Hong Kong's workers are born
elsewhere, and because of waves of political uncertainty, Hong
Kong workers are known for their "visitor" mentality. The lack of a
long-term interest in Hong Kong may contribute to an
unwillingness to invest in specific human capital, and Hong Kong
workers are better endowed in general adaptability than in
specialized skills.

It is also interesting that the fraction of workers who came from
other countries grew steadily from 3% in 1976 to 6% in 1991.
While the reliance on Chinese refugees has diminished, Hong Kong
is drawing more from the international pool of labour. Part of this

Table 2.5
Educational Attainment of the Working Population, 1961–96
(%)

	1961	1971	1981	1991	1996
No schooling / kindergarden	20.1	16.2	10.7	5.6	2.3
Primary	52.7	50.7	36.9	22.9	19.6
Secondary / matriculation	22.9	28.0	45.7	57.4	58.2
Post-secondary / university	4.3	5.1	6.7	14.1	19.9
Mean years of schooling	n.a.	n.a.	7.64	9.25	n.a.

Note: Figures from 1961 to 1991 are based on census reports. Figures for 1996 come from the General Household Survey. Mean years of schooling are calculated from unpublished census files.

pool consists of foreign domestic helpers; another part consists of skilled and well-trained professionals from all over the world.

Many of those workers who were born in China are virtually indistinguishable from native-born workers. It is usually the recent immigrants who face the greatest problems in adapting to the local labour market. Following the immigration wave in the late 1970s, the 1981 census recorded 10% of the workforce as recent immigrants (who had resided in Hong Kong for five or fewer years). By the 1991 census this fraction had fallen to 6%.

One important aspect of labour quality is the level of education of the workforce. The Hong Kong government introduced free and compulsory education at the primary school level in 1971 and extended it to junior secondary education in 1978. Table 2.5 shows that the percentage of the working population with secondary education more than doubled from 1971 to 1991. The proportion of workers with tertiary education also increased — especially since the late 1980s. The percentage rose from 9% in 1986 to 20% in 1996. Calculations based on census data indicate that the average number of years of schooling of the working population increased by almost two years, from 7.4 years in 1976 to 9.3 years 1991.

The education level of the Hong Kong workforce still lags behind that of most developed countries. Given the government

Table 2.6
Percentage Distribution of Working Population by Industry, 1961–96
(%)

Industry	1961	1971	1981	1991	1996
Manufacturing	43.0	47.0	41.3	28.2	18.9
Construction	4.9	5.4	7.7	6.9	8.1
Transport, storage, and communication	7.3	7.4	7.5	9.8	10.9
Wholesale and retail trade, restaurants and hotels	14.4	16.2	24.9	22.5	29.1
Financing, insurance, real estate, and business services	1.6	2.7	4.8	10.6	13.4
Community, social, and personal services	18.3	15.0	15.6	19.9	22.3
Others	10.5	6.3	3.9	2.1	1.5

Note: "Others" include agriculture; fishing; mining and quarrying; electricity, gas, and water; and industries not classifiable. Figures come from various census reports.

policy of expanding university education in Hong Kong, and given the fact that young entrants to the labour force typically have more schooling than old retirees, the trend of rising educational attainment in the workforce is expected to continue.

Sectoral Shifts

In the past few decades the economy of Hong Kong has undergone a series of major structural changes. The post-1949 embargo on China put an abrupt end to entrepôt trade in Hong Kong, and the ensuing rise and decline of manufacturing industries is an often-told story. Within the manufacturing sector, textiles have given way to garments, and plastics have been supplanted by electronics. During the period commerce and financial services continued to grow until Hong Kong eventually emerged as one of the world's financial centres. The reopening of China in the late 1970s accelerated these changes by offering an abundance of cheap labour as well as an abundance of new business opportunities. Outward processing trade with China was almost non-existent in the early 1980s. In

1994 Hong Kong people sent $181 billion worth of raw materials and semi-manufactures into China for processing and received $777 billion worth of processed goods. To put these figures in perspective, the total value added from all domestic manufacturing establishments in that year was $112 billion (Census and Statistics Department 1996). The shift of the manufacturing base to China is unmistakable.

Table 2.6 shows the changes in percentage distribution of employment by industries since 1961. In the 1970s the share of manufacturing employment started to fall. Between 1981 and 1996 the absolute level of employment in the manufacturing sector fell from 990,000 to 575,000. The number of jobs lost from the manufacturing sector alone is about one-fifth the size of the working population. During the same period the employment share in financing, insurance, real estate, and business services more than doubled. The number of new jobs created in these and other sectors far exceeded the number of jobs lost in manufacturing. As a result, unemployment remained below 5% throughout this period.

Changes in broad sectoral shares mask the even more volatile employment fluctuations at finer levels of disaggregation. For example, while manufacturing employment as a whole experienced a significant decline, employment in printing and publishing industries more than doubled during the past 20 years. As another example, repair services showed virtually no growth in a period during which the service sector in general was expanding. The sudden boom and the subsequent bust in wig production is a well-known episode in the history of Hong Kong manufacturing. At its peak in 1970 the wig industry employed more than 30,000 people; currently it hires fewer than 100 (Census and Statistics Department 1993a). Real estates brokerage and agencies had about 2,000 employees in 1984. In 1994 this sector had 17,000 people on its payroll (Census and Statistics Department 1984; 1994). The changes in employment level in some selected industries are displayed in Figure 2.7.

One way to summarize the extent of sectoral shifts is to calculate the following index:

Figure 2.7
Number of Persons Engaged in Selected Industries, 1967–94

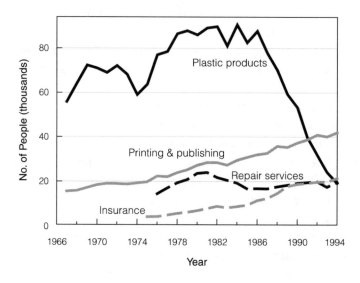

Source: Hong Kong Census and Statistics Department (various years).

$$\frac{1}{2} \sum \left| \; s_i - s'_i \; \right|.$$

In the above formula s_i the employment share of sector i in one year and s'_i is the employment share of the same sector in another year. The absolute value of the change in employment share, $|s_i - s'_i|$, represents the minimum fraction of workers who have left or joined this particular sector in the interim period. Summing these absolute changes across all sectors would give an indication of the mobility of workers necessitated by sectoral shifts. Since workers who leave one sector will join another sector, the overall sum is divided by two to avoid double counting.

Table 2.7 shows the index of sectoral shifts for Hong Kong and for some other countries. During the early 1980s the rate of structural transformation in Hong Kong was below that in Singapore and in South Korea but above that in Japan and in the United States. However, thanks to closer economic links with China, sectoral shifts in Hong Kong accelerated markedly in the late

Table 2.7
Index of Sectoral Shifts, International Comparison for the 1980s

Country	1982–86	1987–92
Hong Kong	**3.58**	**8.90**
Japan	2.05	2.22
Korea, Republic of	8.48	6.50
Singapore	5.98	3.27
United States	2.94	2.16

Source: Wing Suen (1995), "Sectoral Shifts: Impact on Hong Kong Workers," *Journal of International Trade and Economic Development* 4 (July), Table 3.

Note: The index is based on ten broad economic sectors.

1980s. The rate of structural transformation surpassed all these four countries in the period 1987–92.

Another dimension of the transformation of the Hong Kong economy is the change in its occupational structure. Because of a major reclassification of occupation groups, the occupational structures before and after 1991 are not directly comparable. Table 2.8 shows the change in occupational structure between 1976 and 1991 based on a re-coding of unpublished census files. As expected, there was a general upgrading in the distribution of occupations. The proportion of workers who were managers and administrators increased by four percentage points during this period, and the proportion of professionals and associate professionals rose by seven percentage points.

Table 2.8 also shows how the changing distribution of occupations varies across industries. Perhaps the most interesting feature of the table is that the increase in the percentage of managerial and administrative workers (occupation code 1) is higher in the manufacturing sector than in other sectors. Moreover the proportion of clerical workers (code 4) in the manufacturing sector increased substantially, by eight percentage points, while the proportion of direct production workers (codes 7, 8, and 9) fell by twenty-two points. This is consistent with the view that many local manufacturers have moved their production facilities to China and

Table 2.8
Changes in Occupational Structure, 1976–91

Industry	Occupation Code					
	1	2 / 3	4	5	7 / 8	9
Electricity, gas, and water	+1.2	+8.4	–2.8	–1.2	+1.5	–3.5
Manufacturing	+8.0	+5.6	+7.9	+0.6	–27.2	+5.5
Construction	+4.4	+2.7	+1.1	+0.8	–18.5	+10.4
Wholesale and retail trade, restaurants and hotels	–0.1	+3.0	+5.4	–0.3	+0.9	–8.4
Transport, storage, and communication	+4.1	+4.3	+4.8	+2.7	–2.8	–12.8
Financing, insurance, real estate, and business services	+4.1	+13.4	–24.4	–4.9	+5.9	+5.9
Community, social, and personal services	+0.1	+2.9	+1.3	–13.6	-2.3	+13.2
All industries	+4.1	+7.7	+6.3	–0.4	–20.2	+3.0

Source: Wing Suen (1995). "Sectoral Shifts: Impact on Hong Kong Workers," *Journal of International Trade and Economic Development* 4 (July), Table 4.

Note: The numbers refer to the net change in the share of workers in different occupations in each industry. The unit is a percentage point. The occupations are grouped into the following codes: (1) managers and administrators; (2 / 3) professionals and associate professionals; (4) clerks; (5) service workers and shop workers; (7 / 8) craft workers, machine operators, and assemblers; (9) elementary occupations.

now use Hong Kong mainly as a distribution and control centre for their regional operations. This phenomenon is illustrated by the expression "the shop at the front, the factory at the back". Jobs in manufacturing firms in Hong Kong are therefore becoming less production related. The degree of de-industrialization in Hong Kong, then, is greater than that suggested by the decline in total manufacturing employment alone.

The change in occupational structure after 1991 is shown in Table 2.9. Although the time span is relatively short, one can already detect a shift towards more skill-intensive and white-collar occupations. The combined share of managers, administrators, professionals, and associate professionals rose from 23% in 1991 to 28% in 1996. The shares of craft workers, machine operators, and elementary occupations all showed a significant drop.

To what extent will the decline of manufacturing and the rise of services continue in the future? A clue can be obtained from the experience of other city economies. As is shown in Table 2.10, manufacturing employment share is considerably lower in Hong Kong than in Singapore. Part of the reason for this is that the Singapore government deliberately implements policies that favour manufacturing. In the United States, where industrial policy is not widely practised, manufacturing employment share is even lower than that in Hong Kong. The level at which manufacturing employment will stabilize will depend on the future direction of the Hong Kong economy. Shu-ki Tsang (1994) depicts a scenario in which Hong Kong becomes the "Manhattan" of south China. If economic integration with China goes well, the relevant benchmark for the future structure of the Hong Kong economy will not be the United States but New York. Table 2.10 shows that manufacturing employment in New York is below 10% of total employment. Financing, insurance, real estate, and business services comprise a much greater percentage of the workforce in New York than in Hong Kong. Based on this comparison, the structural transformation of the Hong Kong economy does not seem to have reached its end yet.

Labour Earnings and Labour Costs

Hong Kong workers have experienced strong growth in earnings in the past two decades. According to the General Household Survey, median monthly earnings almost tripled from $3,400 in 1976 to $9,900 in 1995 (1995 dollars). Figure 2.8 shows that the growth in real earnings was quite stable over time and was roughly in line with overall economic growth. The annual rate of growth of real GDP per capita in the 1976–91 period was 5.3%, while the rate of growth of real median earnings was 5.5%.

Table 2.9

Percentage Distribution of Working Population by Occupation, 1991 and 1996
(%)

Occupation	1991	1996
Administrative and managerial workers	9.2	12.1
Professionals	3.7	5.0
Associate professionals	10.3	12.1
Clerks	15.9	16.8
Service workers and shop sales workers	13.2	13.8
Craft and related workers	14.7	12.3
Plant and machine operators and assemblers	13.5	8.5
Elementary occupations	18.5	18.6
Others	1.0	0.8

Source: Hong Kong Census and Statistics Department (1997). *1996 Population By-census: Summary Results.* Hong Kong, Government Printer, p. 31, Table 19.

Table 2.10

Employment Shares by Sectors, International Comparison, 1993
(%)

	Hong Kong	Singapore	United States	New York
Agriculture and mining	0.6	0.2	2.7	0.1
Manufacturing	21.3	27.0	16.4	9.6
Construction	7.9	6.4	6.1	1.4
Transport, communication, and public utilities	12.0	11.0	7.1	5.6
Wholesale and retail trade, restaurants and hotels	28.4	22.8	20.8	19.3
Financing, insurance, real estate, and business services	9.6	10.9	10.9	32.7
Community, social, and personal services	20.2	21.6	35.5	31.1

Note: Numbers in the table are percentage shares. Data for Hong Kong, Singapore, and the United States are obtained from the *1994 Yearbook of Labour Statistics.* Information for New York comes from County Business Patterns data of the U.S. Bureau of Economic Analysis.

The rise in earnings can also be observed if we follow a group of workers as they age over time. In Figure 2.9 we plot the average earnings of individuals born in various five-year intervals (the "cohorts"). Individuals born in earlier years were relatively old by the time they appeared in the 1976 census. Despite worsening health and the obsolescence of skills, these earlier cohorts experienced significant improvements in earnings over time. For later cohorts general productivity growth has been accompanied by accumulation of human capital, and earnings growth among these younger cohorts is even more pronounced, as is indicated by the steeper earnings profiles.

It should be pointed out that the earnings growth shown by the General Household Surveys and by the Population Censuses is much stronger than the growth as indicated by various wage and salary indices. For example, the wage index for supervisory, technical, clerical, and miscellaneous non-production workers increased by 28% from 1984 to 1995, while the General Household Survey shows an increase in median earnings of 79% in the same period. This is because earnings data are based on individuals, and wage indices are based on jobs. As an individual progresses from a low-paying job to a high-paying one, his earnings will rise even if the wages for both jobs remain unchanged. For evaluating changes in worker welfare, the earnings data will be appropriate. The wage and salary indices will be useful for analyzing other issues such as changes in labour costs.

Wages or earnings alone, however, cannot tell us whether the workforce is competitive in the world market. Two other factors are important in determining whether labour is "expensive" or "cheap": labour productivity and the non-wage costs of labour. In Hong Kong wages have risen steadily, but so has labour productivity. Figure 2.10 plots the index of real wages (measured by compensation per person) and the index of productivity (measured by value added per person) in manufacturing industries. The two series follow similar trends, although fluctuations in productivity growth are greater than fluctuations in wage growth. During the

Figure 2.8
Growth in Labour Earnings and per capita GDP, 1976–95

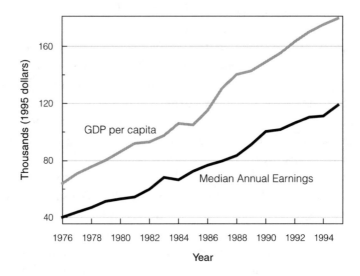

Source: Hong Kong Census and Statistics Department (various years).

period 1976–94, real wage in manufacturing increased at a rate of
4.5% per year, while average productivity increased at a rate of
5.2%. As a result, unit labour cost (total compensation as a fraction
of value added) actually fell slightly from 0.56 to 0.50. As long as
productivity growth remains strong, Hong Kong workers can enjoy
rising wages without losing the competitiveness of their products.

   To employers, wages are only part of the total cost of labour.
Paid holidays, medical benefits, insurance, and various kinds of
employment-related taxes can add substantially to labour cost. Up
to a point, some of these non-wage benefits can be worth more to
the workers than what such benefits cost the employers. For
example, holidays may increase productivity at work, and group
medical insurance is often less expensive than individual policies.
This is why many employers voluntarily offer non-wage benefits to
their employees. However, many governments also impose
mandatory requirements on the level of such benefits. If the
mandated levels are too high, they will generate waste by reducing

Figure 2.9
Earnings Growth by Year of Birth, 1921–25 Cohort to 1961–65 Cohort

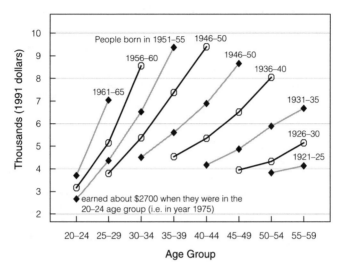

Source: Hong Kong Census and Statistics Department (various years).
Note: People born during 1951–55 are in the 1951–55 "birth cohorts" and their
           earnings are traced in the third track from the left, as illustrated. They earned
           about $9300 Hong Kong dollars in 1991 (in the 35–39 age group).

the scope of workers' choice, and they will reduce employment by increasing employers' labour costs.

An example of inefficient employment benefits in Hong Kong is the housing quarters provided to senior civil servants. When government doctors were given the choice of an equivalent cash allowance in lieu of housing quarters following the establishment of the Hospital Authority, almost all opted for cash. Within the civil service, many also choose the Home Financing Scheme with a substantially lower cash value than government housing quarters. It is clear that a more flexible compensation package (with a larger cash component) can be designed to reduce the government's labour costs without hurting its employees. To be sure, private sector employers are not obliged to offer housing benefits. But the example still illustrates the potential wastes that can arise when the level of in-kind compensation is set too high.

Figure 2.10
Wage, Productivity, and Unit Labour Cost in Manufacturing

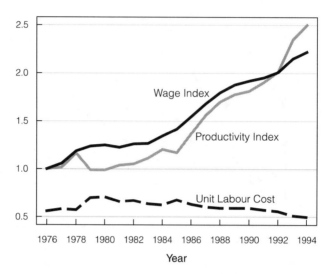

Source: Hong Kong Census and Statistics Department (various years). See text.
Note: Wage Index and Productivity Index for 1976 are set to 1.0. See text.

The Hong Kong government has gradually increased the level of mandated paid holidays, maternity leave, and severance pay over the years. It is currently devising legislation that would require employers and employees to contribute to pension funds. On the whole, however, the level of mandatory non-wage benefits and taxes is still modest by international standards. In 1993 the average monthly salary in manufacturing industries was $6,990. Total compensation per employee was $8,260 per month. Thus wages comprised 82% of labour costs. In comparison, direct wage payment as a fraction of total labour costs was 71% in the United States, 65% in the United Kingdom, and 49% in Germany (International Labour Office 1995). When these four regions are ranked according to their degree of labour market flexibility, Hong Kong usually comes first, Germany is at the bottom, and the United States and the United Kingdom are in between. Perhaps it is no coincidence that they are ranked in the same order according to the proportion of direct wage payment in total labour costs.

In many ways, popular discussions about the "problem" of labour costs are misguided. It is often alleged, especially by business interests, that high wages will reduce the competitiveness of Hong Kong. This statement is logically flawed, because it overlooks the fact that the demand for labour is a derived demand. Employers will not be willing to pay high wages unless workers are highly productive. The statement is also misleading, because it suggests that high wages are something to be avoided. But what is the point of staying competitive if labour does not reap the benefits of competitiveness?

High labour costs are to be dreaded when they do not reflect labour productivity. For example, minimum wage laws will artificially raise the price of labour. Such legislated change in labour costs will reduce the level of employment, and typically low-skilled workers will be hurt most. High labour costs are also to be dreaded when costs to employers do not translate efficiently into benefits for workers. For example, excessive mandatory fringe benefits and other employment levies tend to limit the scope of workers' choice and reduce the level of employment. Luckily for Hong Kong, rising wages have been largely the result of productivity growth, and non-wage payments remain a relatively small fraction of total labour compensation. Such a rise in labour costs need not be dreaded.

Institutional Development

Labour relations in Hong Kong revolve around the employment contract. Collective agreements between trade unions and employers have never played an important part in the labour market. The union density (total declared union membership as a fraction of the number of salaried employees and wage earners) hovered around 16% for most of the 1980s. In the late 1980s the union density began to rise, and it reached 21% in 1995. Most of the increase can be attributed to the growth of membership in civil servants' trade unions (Labour Department 1996). The numerical strength of Hong Kong trade unions, however, belies their ineffectual role in the operation of the labour market.

Turner (1980), England (1989), and many others have commented on how ideological division between Communist and Kuomintang supporters contributes to the fragmentation of local labour movements. More importantly, however, the legal and economic environment in Hong Kong is not conducive to trade union power. Although union activities are protected by law, employers are not required to engage in collective bargaining with labour unions. The highly competitive nature of local industries also limits the ability of labour unions to extract rents. If a trade union successfully negotiates an above-competitive wage for its members, the employer will soon go out of business for failing to constrain costs. In an economy with many outside job opportunities and few investments in firm-specific human capital, workers will often find the "exit" option preferable to raising "voice" with their employers, to use Hirschman's (1970) terminology.

Perhaps the exceptions will prove the rule. Cathay Pacific Airways and the former Hong Kong Cable and Wireless Limited were among the few companies in Hong Kong with strong labour unions. Both companies were shielded from direct competition by government franchises. A well-organized labour union could potentially expropriate part of the monopoly rents from such companies. As another example, the powerful Professional Teachers Union derives some of its strength from the fact that its main employer, the Hong Kong government, has a virtual monopoly in the provision of education. It should also be noted that specific types of human capital are relatively important among teachers and among airline employees. The next best opportunities for such workers are typically much worse than their current employment, and they have a higher-than-average incentive to protect their sunk investments through bargaining rather than through labour turnover.

These few exceptions notwithstanding, the scope for rent sharing with employers is generally limited in Hong Kong. In the United States, one of the primary beneficiaries of airline, railway, and trucking regulations were the employees in these industries. Deregulation in these sectors since the late 1970s has greatly diminished union power and labour earnings (e.g., Rose 1987). Producers in Hong Kong are generally less well protected by the government from open competition, and the ability of labour unions to extract producer rents is diminished as a result.

On the other end of this relationship, the ability of producers to expropriate rents from labour is also limited. An employer may promise an employee high future wages in exchange for investments in firm-specific capital. Once the investments are in place, however, the high wages may not be forthcoming, because the employer knows that these specific investments are not worth much to other employers. One role of labour unions, therefore, is to enforce such implicit contracts and prevent the appropriation of rents by employers (Klein, Crawford, and Alchian 1978). Hong Kong workers, however, are better known for their flexibility than for their firm-specific skills. They are therefore less attached to a particular employer and have less need for union protection against employers' opportunistic behaviour.

The limited scope for bargaining over rents is reflected in the incidence of strikes and industrial actions. Figure 2.11 shows the number of work stoppages and work days lost each year since 1961. The dotted line shows a noticeable decline in work days lost since the 1980s. From 1961 to 1970 the average number of work days lost was 38,500 a year. In the subsequent decade this number fell to 26,000. In the 1981–90 period work days lost due to labour disputes dropped sharply to an average of 5,700 a year, and in 1991–96 the average number of work days lost was 4,000. This drop is more remarkable considering that the size of the Hong Kong labour force has grown more than 150% in these three and a half decades.

To put these numbers in a different perspective, Table 2.11 shows the number of strikes and work days lost per thousand employees in a number of selected countries. The low incidence of industrial action in Canada and the United States is deceiving, as the records for these two countries only include strikes involving more

Figure 2.11
Work Stoppages and Work Days Lost, 1961–96

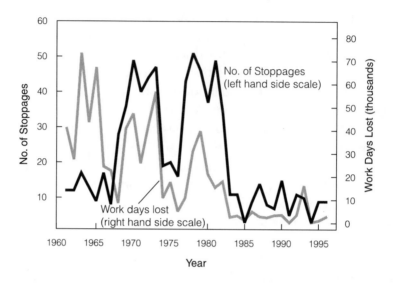

Source: Hong Kong Labour Department (various years).

than 500 workers (for Canada) and more than 1,000 workers (for the United States). The number of work days lost due to labour disputes in Hong Kong is several orders of magnitude lower than that in other countries. Industrial actions in Hong Kong are uncommon and seldom occur on a large scale.

Government Involvement in the Labour Market

While the economic environment of Hong Kong has not been — and is not — favourable to union power in the labour market, the political environment has slowly shifted in favour of more representation of union interests in the legislative arena. What cannot be achieved via industrial action or collective bargaining can sometimes be accomplished by the government, and trade unions are more and more frequently making use of this avenue to reach their goals.

Table 2.11

Strikes and Work Days Lost per thousand Employees, 1994*

	Strikes	Work days lost
Canada*	0.0025	49.9
France	0.0616	24.2
Germany*	n.a.	19.9
Hong Kong	**0.0010**	**0.1**
India	0.0688	1,258.1
Japan	0.0051	4.5
Korea, Republic of	0.0123	111.3
Sweden	0.0033	13.3
United Kingdom*	0.0098	30.1
United States*	0.0003	33.4

Source: International Labour Office (1995). 1995 *Yearbook of Labour Statistics. Geneva: International Labour Office.*

Note: *Figures refer to 1994 or latest. Data for Germany and United Kingdom records strikes involving at least 100 lost workdays. Data for Canada excludes strikes involving fewer than 500 workers, and data for the United States excludes strikes involving fewer than 1000 workers.

The largest alliance of labour unions in Hong Kong is the Federation of Trade Unions. In the 1960s and 1970s the Federation of Trade Unions was mostly absorbed by internal politics in China and was not directly involved in the formulation of local labour policies. It was not until 1981 that the Federation of Trade Unions began to participate in the elections to choose employees' representatives on the Labour Advisory Board, the government consultative committee responsible for labour policies in Hong Kong (England 1989). In 1985 trade unions gained two seats in the Legislative Council as the government introduced indirect elections through "functional constituencies". During this period, however, trade unions still had a minority voice in the policy making process. Their role is more accurately described as that of pressure groups.

A more significant development was the creation of 18 directly-elected seats (which were later increased to 20 seats) in the Legislative Council in 1991. With salaried workers and wage earners making up almost 90% of the labour force, the potential

Figure 2.12
Expenditure of the Labour Department, 1961–96

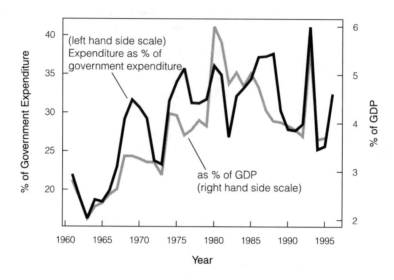

Source: Hong Kong Labour Department (various years).

block of votes they can deliver cannot be ignored. After the 1995 elections nine out of the sixty Legislative Council members had some union background, and legislators of every stripe claimed to speak for labour interests. To what extent such political changes will translate into labour legislations will remain to be seen.

The principal piece of labour legislation in Hong Kong is the Employment Ordinance. The Employment Ordinance was first enacted in 1968. In the ensuing 25 years 335 items of new or amended labour legislation governing industrial safety, conditions of employment, and the protection of wages on insolvency were introduced (Labour Department 1992). The Employment Ordinance is now applicable to all employees irrespective of their earnings. It lays down provisions for employment conditions such as annual leave, maternity leave, severance pay, and long-service pay. The Labour Department is responsible for enforcing labour legislations, and it also assists in matters such as mediating labour disputes, providing placement service, and promoting industrial health and safety. An important innovation was the creation of the Labour Tribunal in 1972. The Tribunal has jurisdiction over "claims of entitlement to a sum of money arising from the breach of an existing contract of employment" (Williams 1990). Hearings at the Labour Tribunal are usually conducted in Cantonese. Contending parties will make statements themselves without legal representation, and the tribunal can make its own investigations. In a place where law courts are clogged by case overload, where attorney fees are maintained by professional cartels, and where legal procedures are almost entirely based on a foreign language, the Labour Tribunal may be the only feasible recourse to justice for many ordinary workers.

Figure 2.12 shows the annual expenditure of the Labour Department as a fraction of total government expenditure (solid line) and as a fraction of GDP (dotted line). The graphs show slight but erratic growth in the relative size of the Labour Department. Most of the expansion occurred during the 1960s, when the Employment Ordinance was beginning to be put in place. This is consistent with the view that the Employment Ordinance is the keystone piece of labour legislation in Hong Kong.

It is, however, difficult to measure the extent to which government legislations have actually affected the operation of the labour market. Departmental expenditure is misleading because most of the costs of government intervention do not directly show up in the budget. For example, regulations regarding annual leave and long-service pay are borne by the contracting parties. Moreover, regulations raising the mandated benefits may merely be codification of existing practices, just as wages have increased without direct intervention from the government. Some regulations may even be efficiency enhancing, as the state is sometimes a more cost-effective enforcer of implicit or explicit labour contracts than private parties. On the whole, the degree of government intervention in the labour market is modest compared to that in Western developed countries. The government does not set minimum wages (except in the case of some foreign imported workers); workers do not receive unemployment benefits (though unemployed people can apply for public assistance subject to a means test); and there is no unemployment insurance tax.

With the recent changes in the political and legislative environment, there is a movement towards more activist labour policies. Legislation for a mandatory pension scheme has been put in place, and an unfair dismissal law is under consideration. An Equal Opportunity Commission was set up in 1995 to deal with, among other things, equal opportunity in employment. It is difficult to predict how these policies will evolve, as the 1997 transition will certainly affect the political parameters under which labour market policies are formulated. In Chapter 5 we will take a closer look at some of the policy options for the labour market at this juncture of institutional change.

CHAPTER 3

The Market at Work

It is a straightforward exercise in economic theory to show that, under certain assumptions, a competitive labour market will lead to an optimal allocation of human resources. It is equally straightforward, however, to imagine institutional features of the labour market that seem to undermine the competitive assumptions. Although the Hong Kong labour market is relatively free from the visible hands of the government, one can never conclusively establish that the market is perfectly competitive. For example, H. A. Turner (1980) argues in an influential study that the Hong Kong labour market is far from the competitive model, although his view is disputed by Alan Stretton (1981) and by L. C. Chau (1988), among others. In this chapter we refrain from argument about assumptions; instead we examine how the market has actually worked.

The preceding chapter outlined the major developments in various aspects of the labour market in Hong Kong. Just like any other market, the labour market is constantly subject to exogenous changes in demand and supply. How well it works is best assessed by studying how it responds to these changes in the environment. In this chapter we select three broad changes and their labour market effects for detailed analysis: the entry of women into the labour force, immigration, and sectoral shifts.

These three areas are among the core issues of the Hong Kong labour market. Thanks to the release of random sub-samples from the population censuses, a number of econometric studies have emerged recently that carefully document the labour market effects of immigration, sectoral shifts, and women's entry into the labour force. Such quantitative studies allow us to go beyond verbal arguments about the competitiveness of the labour market towards a more precise understanding of the market in action. We do not suggest that these three issues are the only or the most important ones in the labour market of Hong Kong, but they are the best understood. Other labour market problems are less well understood because of the lack of evidence. Nonetheless, these other problems also pose potential challenges for Hong Kong and cannot be ignored. They will be examined in Chapter 4.

In our discussion of women in the labour market we will show how female labour force participation decisions are affected by economic incentives. We will also show how the market rewards the rising labour market experience of women. The chapter will then describe how immigrants are assimilated into the local labour market and analyze the effects of immigration on wages and employment. In the section on sectoral shifts, we will study their effects on the wage structure and on unemployment. Putting the experience from these three examples together, a broad picture will emerge in which:

1. Economic incentives do matter in the labour market;
2. Wages reflect productivity and respond to demand and supply conditions as economic theory says they do; and
3. The labour market is flexible enough to avoid high unemployment in the face of demand and supply shocks.

These themes will be elaborated upon in the remainder of the chapter.

The Entry of Women into the Labour Force

The secular increase in female labour force participation since World War II is perhaps the single most important labour market trend to have taken place in Hong Kong as well as in many other countries. The previous chapter pointed out some of the demographic and social factors behind this change. However, female labour force participation is still far from universal among married women. According to recent General Household Surveys about 60% of all married women in Hong Kong choose to stay out of the labour force. What explains the variations in labour market status across women?

The decision to join or to stay out of the labour market can be viewed as a problem in the optimal allocation of time. Participation in the labour market reduces the time available for leisure and other home activities, but it also increases the income available for purchasing consumption goods. The terms of this trade-off are given by the market wage rates. Women facing a higher wage rate also face a higher price of leisure, and they are more likely to participate in market work. This is known as the "substitution effect". On the other hand, women with larger non-wage incomes (such as income from the spouse) will have a higher demand for leisure time, and they will be less likely to participate in market work. This is known as the "income effect".

In an earlier work Suen (1996), estimates a model of the determinants of labour participation among married women using 1991 census data. According to that model, a 10% increase in the predicted wage of a woman will raise the probability of her labour participation from 0.43 to 0.55. This powerful substitution effect stands in contrast to a relatively weak income effect: it is estimated that a $1,000 increase in non-wage income (which amounts to roughly an 8% increase) will reduce the participation probability by only one percentage point.

The effect of market wage rates on labour force participation are clearly depicted in Figure 3.1. This figure shows the running average of the labour force participation rate against the predicted wage of married women (the wage variable is imputed from a regression model). Although the relationship is not smooth and linear, the generally positive response of female labour supply to market wage is evident.

At the individual level, the high degree of responsiveness of female labour supply to market wage suggests that economic incentives are an important consideration in people's labour market

Figure 3.1
Effect of Wage on Labour Participation, Moving Average Estimates

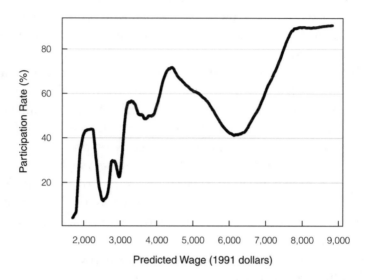

Predicted Wage (1991 dollars)

Source: Unpublished census files.

decisions. At the aggregate level, this high wage elasticity will contribute to increasing the flexibility of the labour market. Many (but by no means all) women are second earners in the family, and they are more ready than men to move in and out of the labour force in response to market opportunities. For example, a temporary increase in labour demand can in part be met by drawing non-working women into employment. This additional source of labour supply elasticity has the effect of relieving bottlenecks and moderating fluctuations in wages.

Whereas individuals base their participation decisions on market wages, market wages will also respond to people's participation decisions. This is because there is an investment aspect to labour force participation. Work experience in the labour market tends to enhance productivity through on-the-job training and learning-by-doing. People with greater labour market experience generally earn more than do those with less experience until obsolescence and poor health intervene at old age. The gap between male and female earnings is at least partly attributable to the difference in their actual labour market experience (Mincer and Polachek 1974).

In Hong Kong the female labour force participation rate increased steadily until the second half of the 1980s. In a well-functioning labour market, the rising market experience of women will translate into a narrower gender wage gap. This is precisely what happened. From 1976 to 1986 the female labour force participation rate grew from 44% to 51%, and the female-male earnings ratio also grew from 0.63 to 0.73. From 1986 to 1991, when the female participation rate hardly changed, the earnings gap also remained stable (Lui and Suen 1993; Suen 1995c).

One alternative explanation of the difference between men's and women's wages is labour market discrimination. While discrimination may be present in varying degrees, it explains neither the variations in the wage gap across age groups nor the changes in wage rates over time. Figure 3.2 is reproduced from Suen (1995c). Panel (a) shows the close concordance between differential labour force participation and differential earnings for each age group between 15 and 65. The earnings gap between men and women is most pronounced for prime age workers, and so is the participation gap. In the younger age groups, male and female labour force participation rates are not that different, and the gender wage gap is also small. In fact, the simple correlation coefficient of these two variables is 0.86. Panel (b) shows that between 1986 and 1991, the female labour force participation rate rose for the younger age groups but fell for the older groups. During the same period, the earnings increased faster for younger female workers than they did for older workers. The simple correlation between the change in female labour participation and the change in female earnings is 0.29. These findings are entirely consistent with human capital theory. Proponents of discrimination theory would have to concoct very clever stories to explain the patterns shown in Figure 3.2.

Historically women have been at a disadvantaged position in the labour market. The labour market in Hong Kong, however, does show sufficient flexibility to reward work and experience. As

Chapter 3

Figure 3.2
Labour Force Participation and Earnings: Gender Differences

(a) Participation and Earning Differences, Men vs Women, 1991

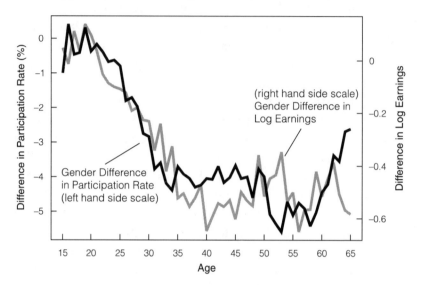

(b) Changes in Participation and Earnings, Female, 1986–91

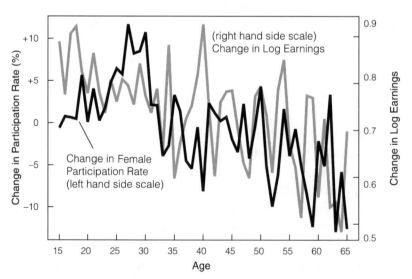

Source: Wing Suen (1995), "Gender Gap in Hong Kong: An Update," *Asian Economic Journal* 9 (November), Figure 3.

more and more women have entered the labour force and accumulated labour market experience, their disadvantage has begun to erode. The goodwill of employers and legislators might help further decrease this disadvantage, but women's continued progress will ultimately depend on their increasing commitment and attachment to the workforce.

Immigrants and the Labour Market

New immigrants in any society face numerous problems in the labour market. Job searches depend on social networks and local knowledge, which may not be available to immigrants. The qualifications and skills obtained in their home country may be less valuable in the host country. Proficiency in language cannot be taken for granted. Added to these problems are the hostility and discrimination that plague many immigrants. It is not then very surprising that immigrant earnings are typically lower than are the earnings of native workers.

A well-functioning labour market, however, will not let temporary problems crystallize into permanent handicaps. Immigrants, who have to bear the high costs of dislocation, are usually a highly motivated group. When given the chance, many are willing to make extra sacrifices to improve their human capital. Such efforts are not futile in a market that rewards merit rather than origin. In fact, one of the hallmarks of a flexible labour market (and of an open society for that matter) is the rapid assimilation of immigrants.

One way to study the assimilation of immigrants is to compare the earnings of newly arrived immigrants to that of those who arrived earlier. If we ignore systematic differences in the quality of different immigrant cohorts, the difference in their earnings can be attributed to the assimilation effect (Chiswick 1978; see also Borjas 1985). Based on unpublished 1991 census data, we compute the average earnings of Chinese immigrants with different numbers of years of residence in Hong Kong. The results are shown in Figure 3.3. For men, those who arrived in Hong Kong five to nine years ago

Figure 3.3
Immigrant Earnings by Duration of Residence

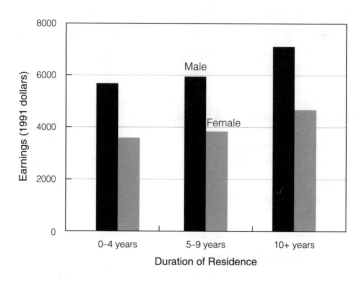

Source: Unpublished census files.

earned 5% more than those who arrived zero to four years ago, and those who have been in Hong Kong for ten or more years in turn had an earnings premium of 19% over the former group. The pattern for women is similar.

In a more detailed study Kit-chun Lam and Pak-wai Liu (1993) use regression analysis to estimate the rate of assimilation of immigrants. After controlling for differences in education and experience, they find that immigrants who have stayed in Hong Kong one more year earn 1.9% more than comparable immigrants who have not stayed the additional year. Although immigrants still earn systematically less than natives do, much of the difference in earnings can be attributed to the inferior education received by immigrants in China (Lui and Suen 1996). For example, immigrants who have received at least part of their education in Hong Kong enjoy a higher rate of return to schooling than those who completed their education in China. We do not suggest that immigrants face no problem adapting to Hong Kong; but with time and effort they have a good chance of improving their position in the labour market.

Sadly, the public has shown less concern about the well-being of immigrants than about the potential impact of immigrants on native workers. The perceived threat to local workers is often based on instinct (recall the "fallacy of scarce jobs") than on analysis or evidence. Empirical studies in the United States usually find a small negative effect of immigration on employment, with estimated elasticity that range from –0.01 (Borjas 1990) to –0.06 (Altonji and Card 1991). These are very weak effects. The meaning of –0.06 is that a 10% increase in the stock of immigrants (a relatively large change) is expected to reduce the employment of native workers by not more than 0.6%. Research concerning the effect of immigration on the unemployment rate is even more inconclusive. The estimated elasticity range from –0.01 (Muller and Espenshade 1985) to +0.01 (Simon, Moore, and Sullivan 1993).

While the U.S. experience cannot be directly applied to Hong Kong, it suggests that immigration does not generally have a substantial impact on the local labour market. Data in Hong Kong are too coarse to permit a rigorous analysis. We calculate the net arrival rate (the rate of population growth minus the rate of natural increase) as a proxy for the rate of immigration. The relationship between the net arrival rate and the unemployment rate in the period 1976–1996 is shown in Figure 3.4. The correlation between these two variables is only 0.15, and this weak relationship cannot be statistically distinguished from zero correlation. For example, the huge immigration wave in 1979 produced a net arrival rate of 4.4%; yet the unemployment rate of 2.9% in 1979 was only 0.05 percentage points above average.

It is perhaps not surprising that immigration has little effect on unemployment. After all, immigrants increase the demand as well as the supply of labour. A more plausible effect of immigration on the labour market works through changes in factor proportions. If immigrants possess less capital than the natives do, as is usually the case, then an increase in immigration will lower the capital-labour ratio, which will in turn lower the price of labour. In reality the

Figure 3.4
Relation between Immigration and Unemployment, 1976–96

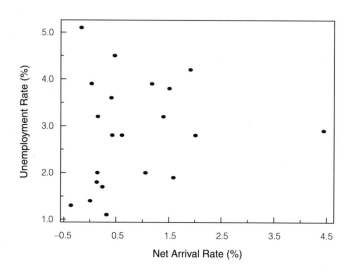

Source: Hong Kong Census and Statistics Department (various years).

situation is a bit more complex, as immigrants may be substitutes to some types of labour (e.g., unskilled labour) and complements to other types (e.g., skilled labour). For example, having more typists may increase the productivity, and hence the wage, of managers but decrease the wage of fellow typists. The actual wage effect will also depend on the degree of economies of scale. If there are strong economies of scale, the scale effect may offset the factor-proportions effect to result in an increase in the price of labour.

Research in the United States typically finds a very small effect of immigration on the wages of natives. In an influential study, LaLonde and Topel (1991) estimate that a 10% increase in the number of immigrants in a city will lower the local wages of young blacks and Hispanic Americans by at most 0.1%. Summarizing the conclusions from a number of empirical studies, Borjas (1990, p. 81) states that, "the methodological arsenal of modern econometrics cannot detect a single shred of evidence that immigrants have a sizable adverse impact on the earnings and employment opportunities of natives in the United States."

Most studies in the United States are based on comparing cities with large immigrant population to cities with small immigrant population. This type of approach is obviously not applicable to Hong Kong. In a 1994 study Suen tries to estimate the effect of immigration by exploiting the fact that the proportion of immigrants in different age groups are quite different. If there are more immigrants in the younger age groups, and if immigration adversely affects natives' wages, then the differential impact will be greater for younger natives than it will be for older natives. Using a framework that allows for imperfect substitution between young and old workers as well as between immigrants and natives, Suen finds a statistically significant, but quantitatively small, effect of immigration on wages. For example, Table 3.1 shows the estimated effects of increasing the number of recent immigrants by 40%. Comparing the different columns, it can be seen that increased immigration tends to reduce the wages of young workers relatively more than it reduces the wages of old workers. This reflects the fact that new immigrants are predominantly young. Comparing across rows, one can see that the effects of immigration mainly fall on other immigrants rather than on the native workers. The first row of Table 3.1 shows that the effects on native wages are negative but extremely small. The elasticity range from −0.002 for young natives to −0.0005 for old natives. Most of the impact will be felt by existing recent immigrants. But even for the latter group, the impact is not substantial, with estimated elasticity of about −0.02.

Compared to the entry of women into the labour force, immigration is only a secondary factor in the growth of the labour force. Just as the market has accommodated the increased female labour participation without much adverse effect on men, the impact of immigrants on native earnings and employment has been very small. We believe the focus on the potential threat of immigration may have been misplaced by some groups of people. In our view, more attention should be paid to finding ways to absorb the

Table 3.1
Effect of a 40% Increase in Recent Immigrants on Wages

| | Age group | | | | |
Affected groups	15–24	25–34	35–44	45–54	55–64
Natives	−.077	−.033	−.029	−.030	−.019
	(.024)	(.011)	(.010)	(.010)	(.007)
Immigrants (≥ 7 years)	−.077	−.033	−.029	−.030	−.019
	(.024)	(.011)	(.010)	(.010)	(.007)
Immigrants (< 7 years)	−.718	−.674	−.670	−.670	−.660
	(.290)	(.297)	(.298)	(.298)	(.299)

Source: Wing Suen (1995). "Estimating the Effects of Immigration in One City,"
          Working paper (August), Table 3.
Note: All numbers are in percentage points. Standard errors are in parentheses.

immigrants so that they can quickly become productive members of society.

Sectoral Reallocation of Labour

Until the eighteenth century agriculture was often believed to be more "fundamental" than were other economic activities. The French physiocrats, for example, thought that farming was the only true source of prosperity. In ancient China agriculture carried a higher social status than industry or commerce. With the onset of the industrial revolution, the belief in the primacy of agriculture was gradually replaced by a belief in the primacy of the factory.

Today, in Hong Kong as well as elsewhere, there is still a widespread feeling that manufacturing is the source of national wealth and that manufacturing jobs are somehow "better" than other jobs. This misconception should be dispelled. In most developed countries, manufacturing employment reached its peak 20 or 30 years ago and has been falling steadily in relative terms ever since. None of the major "industrialized" countries has over half of its workforce being in the manufacturing sector. More than 70% of workers in Australia, Britain, Canada, and the United States are employed in the service sector. Hong Kong, like every other developed country, is definitely moving towards a service economy.

Changes in the structure of the economy necessitate a constant reallocation of human resources across industry sectors. Such sectoral reallocation is part of the process of economic growth. It should not — and cannot — be resisted. To save manufacturing jobs would go against global shifts in production and consumption patterns. Manufacturing jobs are not inherently "better" than services jobs, either. Service workers are commonly stereotyped as low skilled and poorly paid. The image is typified by the supermarket checkout clerk and the hamburger flipper. In fact, less than a quarter of the service jobs in Hong Kong are in restaurants or the retail sector (Census and Statistics Department 1996). The fastest-growing service jobs are in business and financial services rather than in personal or social services. Using payroll data from 1993 we calculate that 68% of all service workers earned wages higher than the average manufacturing wage. With increasing integration with China and with liberalization of international trade on the rise, Hong Kong workers will find it more difficult to compete in low-skilled manufacturing jobs. Enthusiasm for "hi-tech" industries notwithstanding, high-skilled jobs are more likely to be found in service than in manufacturing. Adapting to the shift away from manufacturing will ultimately pay the transitional costs.

As workers move away from low-pay sectors towards high-pay sectors, human resources are getting more efficiently utilized. This will cause average labour productivity and labour earnings to rise. To illustrate this effect, let us suppose manufacturing workers make up 40% of total employment while the remaining 60% are in service industries. Suppose further, without deviating too much from the facts, that wages in the manufacturing industry are $9,000 per month and wages in the service industry are $10,000. The overall average wage is then $9,600. If employment in the manufacturing sector declines by half to 20%, then the overall average wage will grow to $9,800, *even if wages in each sector remain unchanged.* According to an earlier calculation based on census data with 25 industries (Suen 1995b), the reallocation of labour alone had contributed to a twelve-percentage-point increase in real earnings in the 1976–91 period, or nearly one-seventh of the total growth in earnings. Using another set of data from the Survey of Employment, Vacancies and Payroll, we update this calculation for the period 1980–93 with a more detailed industry classification (46 industry sectors). We find that average real payroll per person had risen by 66% during that period. Even if real wages in each of the 46 sectors had remained unchanged, the changing composition of labour across the sectors alone would have resulted in an increase in the average real payroll per person of 19%. This suggests that the composition effect may have accounted for as much as two-sevenths of the overall growth in earnings. The labour composition effect may not be noticeable to individual workers in the short term, but the substantial rise in overall earnings *is* the single most important consequence of sectoral labour reallocation in Hong Kong.

Concern over sectoral shifts in Hong Kong has focused primarily on the problems of labour market mismatch and structural unemployment. David Lilien (1982) offers some evidence for the relationship between sectoral shifts and unemployment in the United States. His empirical findings, however, are disputed by Abraham and Katz (1986) and by Murphy and Topel (1987). Recently William Chan (1996) constructed a model of short-run adjustments which shows that the theoretical relationship between sectoral shifts and unemployment is not necessarily positive. In Hong Kong the relevant time series are too short to allow for a detailed investigation. We plot the aggregate unemployment rate from 1982 to 1994 against the index of sectoral shifts (defined in Chapter 2) based on 46 industries. The resulting Figure 3.5 does not suggest any positive relationship between the rate of sectoral shifts and the level of unemployment.

In a more disaggregated analysis, Wing Suen (1995b) studies data on the industry-specific unemployment rates for four broad sectors: manufacturing; construction; wholesale, retail, restaurants

Figure 3.5
Relation between Sectoral Shifts and Unemployment, 1982–94

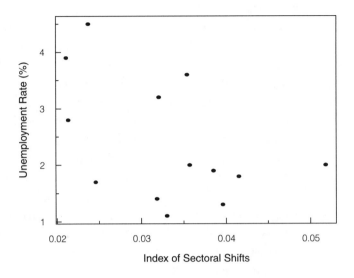

Source: Hong Kong Census and Statistics Department (various years).

and hotels; and services. Using quarterly data for the period 1983–93, he estimates a model in which the industry-specific unemployment rate depends on lagged unemployment and on change in employment share. While past unemployment has a significant effect on current unemployment, the effect of change in employment share is statistically and substantively insignificant. In other words, sectors that experience a greater drop in employment shares do not exhibit higher unemployment rates. More recent data, however, seem to suggest that unemployment rose faster in the manufacturing sector than in other sectors during the economic slowdown of 1995. Chapter 4 will discuss this worrisome trend in greater detail.

Suen (1995b) also finds that the relationship between employment growth and earnings growth is weak. According to his estimate, sectors which experience a one percentage point increase in employment share (which corresponds to a 25% increase in relative employment level) exhibit only a 1.8% higher growth in earnings. If changes in employment shares are the result of changes in labour demand, the implied elasticity of labour supply (to an industry) is about fourteen. When there is a fall in demand for garment workers, for example, their wages will fall. The magnitude of the wage reduction will depend on the elasticity of labour supply to the garment industry. If garment workers do not have many other options, their wages will have to fall substantially before some workers will leave the industry. On the other hand, if workers are relatively mobile across industries, their labour supply to the garment industry will be highly elastic. A slight reduction in wages in the garment sector is sufficient to induce workers to leave and therefore restore the balance between labour supply and labour demand. The evidence suggests that Hong Kong workers are highly mobile across industries, so that large shifts in labour demand are associated with only minor changes in relative wages. The concern over a permanently depressed sector in which workers are stuck with stagnant wages is probably premature.

Although the structural transformation of the Hong Kong economy has not significantly affected relative wages across industries, there is some evidence that relative wages across skill levels have changed. As the economy becomes more sophisticated, tasks that require raw labour power can often been accomplished by machines. At the same time, the increasing use of physical capital induces a greater demand for skilled labour to manage and co-ordinate the production processes. The rise in demand for skilled relative to unskilled labour is partly reflected in an increase in demand for education and partly reflected in an increase in relative wages for skilled workers. In Figure 3.6 we show the real wage index for three class of workers. Real wage growth for craftsmen and operatives clearly lags behind wage growth for non-productive workers and for managers and professionals. Because the level of wages for craftsmen and operatives is below that of other workers, the differential wage growth also means an increasing disparity in wages.

In Table 3.2 we provide direct evidence that the level of wage inequality has increased. Panel (a) shows that the Gini coefficient

Figure 3.6
Wage and Salary Indices, 1974–95

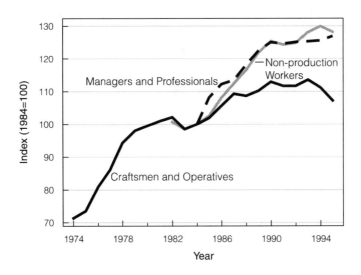

Source: Hong Kong Census and Statistics Department (various years).

for male employment earnings rose from 0.39 in 1976 to 0.43 in 1991. Other measures of earnings inequality tell a similar story. For example, the standard deviation of log earnings has increased from 0.64 to 0.70, and the gap between the tenth percentile earnings and median earnings has increased by roughly 22 percentage points. The measures in panel (c) are based on the residuals from human capital earnings regressions. They indicate that, after controlling for observable characteristics such as education and experience, there is still a trend towards greater earnings inequality.

The trend towards increasing wage inequality has been observed in the United States and in other countries (e.g., Green, Coder, and Ryscavage 1992; Juhn, Murphy, and Pierce 1993; Blau and Kahn 1996). It is part of a global phenomenon involving a shift in demand from relatively unskilled labour to more skilled labour. In countries such as Norway, where wage setting is highly centralized and labour market institutions are highly rigid, the demand shift has resulted in increased unemployment for the

Table 3.2
Measures of Earnings Inequality, 1976–91

	1976	1981	1986	1991
(a) Raw earnings				
Gini coefficient	.386	.382	.410	.427
(b) Log earnings				
standard deviation	.637	.622	.666	.698
90 - 50 percentile	.811	.752	.833	.916
50 - 10 percentile	.470	.552	.693	.693
75 - 25 percentile	.606	.672	.693	.750
(c) Earnings residuals				
standard deviation	.492	.499	.515	.532
90 - 50 percentile	.526	.535	.545	.581
50 - 10 percentile	.545	.574	.620	.615
75 - 25 percentile	.519	.523	.545	.571

Source: Wing Suen (1995), "Sectoral Shifts: Impact on Hong Kong Workers," *Journal of International Trade and Economic Development* 4 (July), Table 7.

unskilled. In places such as the United States and Hong Kong, where wage setting is decentralized and labour markets are flexible, the change has not increased the level of unemployment. Instead the bulk of the adjustments occur through changes in the wage structure. There is, however, one crucial difference between the experience of Hong Kong and the experience of the United States: whereas real wages for low-wage jobs in the United States fell in absolute terms, real wages at all levels in Hong Kong increased sharply. For example, real earnings at the tenth percentile of the distribution in Hong Kong rose 39% between 1981 and 1991, even though they fell by 19% relative to the median. Although the concern about rising wage inequality in Hong Kong is legitimate, it is important to avoid allowing changes in relative earnings to mask the growth in actual earnings.

Wage Flexibility

Underlying the flexibility of the labour market is a self-adjusting mechanism that operates through movements in wages. Institution-alized wage rigidities such as union contracts and the minimum wage are virtually non-existent in Hong Kong. The annual civil service pay increase is perhaps the most elaborate ritual in the Hong Kong labour market. Yet even the government pays attention to current market conditions in setting its wages. The civil service makes up less than 10% of the working population. In the rest of the economy, changes in wages and benefits are subject to few laws except those of supply and demand.

In the previous sections we provide some microeconomics evidence of how wages respond to market conditions. For example, the wages of women and immigrants have improved as these groups have accumulated more relevant labour market experience; the relative earnings of workers at different age groups have changed as the supply changes due to immigration; and the relative earnings of workers in different industries have changed as sectoral labour demand shifts. At the aggregate level, changes in the real wage have also proven to be quite responsive to macroeconomics conditions. Figure 3.7 illustrates.

Figure 3.7 shows the rate of change of real GDP and the rate of change of the real wage index for craftsmen and operatives in various years between 1975 and 1995. A line of best fit is added to the diagram to emphasize the positive relationship between the two variables. This relationship is statistically significant, although the two series cover only a relatively short span of some twenty years. The slope of the line in Figure 3.7 is 0.44, meaning that a one percentage point increase in the rate of GDP growth will raise the rate of real wage growth by 0.44 percentage points on average. In years of strong economic growth, when aggregate labour demand is high, real wages are bid up at a faster rate. When economic growth slackens, wage growth also decelerates and may even become negative. These adjustments help maintain the balance between labour demand and labour supply in face of economic fluctuations.

A closer look at Figure 3.7 also reveals that real wage cuts are not uncommon in Hong Kong. During the recent economic slowdown in 1995, for example, real wages for craftsmen and operatives fell by 4%. In the 1975–95 period there were four years in which real wages registered negative growth, and one year in

Figure 3.7
Relation between GDP Growth and Wage Growth, 1975–95

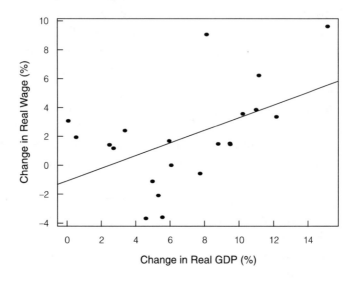

Source: Hong Kong Census and Statistics Department (various years).

which real wages registered zero growth. With a moderately high inflation rate, real wage decreases can be achieved without nominal wage cuts. Such wage cuts are of course painful to workers, but they also help restore the employment level. The flexibility of wages is one of the reasons that Hong Kong has managed to maintain a consistently low level of unemployment for the past twenty years.

CHAPTER 4

New Challenges in a New Era

In the previous two chapters, we have painted, in broad strokes, a picture of the evolving labour market in Hong Kong. What we have seen is a dynamic and flexible labour market driven by economic forces that has adapted remarkably well to a constantly changing environment. In fact, since Hong Kong has virtually no natural endowments except for its harbour and its strategic location, its labour force can be considered the cornerstone of its economy. That Hong Kong has successfully weathered numerous challenges and has emerged as one of the fastest-growing economies in the world is a tribute to the resilience and adaptability of its labour force.

Yet, for all its successes, the Hong Kong economy in general, and the labour market in particular, have suffered their share of growing pains. A small open economy like Hong Kong is always vulnerable to shocks imported from the global economy. Perhaps the single most important variable, internal or external, that has changed Hong Kong's course in the past two decades has been the opening of Chinese economy and the economic and political integration of Hong Kong into China. The new source of cheap labour north of the border decisively shifted the comparative advantage of Hong Kong relative to its trading partners and ushered in a dramatic structural transformation of the Hong Kong economy. Even though, as was explained in the last chapter, the overall labour market has coped very well, the drastic sectoral shifts could not but create some mismatch in the supply of and demand for labour in certain sectors. Thus, while employers in some expanding sectors

complain about chronic labour shortages, high turnover, and spiralling wages, workers in some declining industries become
redundant and experience difficulties in pursuing alternative
careers. The various affected parties' discontent eventually finds
expression in political demands for government intervention. Such
intervention may range from short-term remedial measures to
long-term planning and management of human resources. The
accelerated democratization of the Hong Kong government in the
aftermath of the Tiananmen tragedy only serves to bring this political struggle for economic rent to the fore.

In this chapter, we shall take a closer look beneath the reassur-
ing surface and offer a diagnosis of the potential problems in the
Hong Kong labour market. We shall try to assess the scope and the
extent of these problems and outline the challenges that lie ahead as
Hong Kong enters a new era. The discussion will provide the basis
for evaluating policy options on labour resources in the following
chapter.

Structural Unemployment and Displaced Workers

The positive relationship between unemployment and sectoral
shifts is intuitive. As is explained in Lilien (1982), the structural
transformation of an economy is associated with reallocation of
workers among sectors. This not only raises the incidence of job
separations, but, in a world of uncertainty, also results in more
extensive job search activities in the labour market, because workers are not familiar with the industries they are moving into. In addition, sectoral shifts can also destroy a significant amount of human
capital stock, as skills are often industry-specific and become use-
less once workers are made redundant in their original industries.
And without the necessary training, displaced workers may have
difficulty securing employment in other sectors. All of these factors
can contribute to higher measured unemployment. Indeed, the
media abounds with stories of middle-aged and older displaced
workers who fall into long-term financial hardship as a result of
their reduced employability. Inflated unemployment statistics compiled by pressure groups and unions and widely reported upon in

the local press reinforce the picture of a gravely sick labour market in dire need of a strong dose of government intervention (or of the withdrawal of government initiatives, as in the case of labour importation).

Yet, intuitive as it may seem, the sectoral shift hypothesis has not always been supported by empirical evidence. Murphy and Topel's (1990) study of the evolution of unemployment in the United States in the 1970s and 1980s shows that short-term layoffs, rather than permanent separations and intersectoral mobility, accounted for most of the unemployment spells during periods of extensive sectoral shifts. In Hong Kong, even though the recent economic slowdown pushed official unemployment figures to a twenty-year high of 3.6% in August 1996, the economy has started to rebound, and unemployment is now on the decline. By January 1997 the unemployment rate was down to 2.5%. This recent flair-up of unemployment has more to do with cyclical fluctuations than with sectoral shifts. Nevertheless, this does not mean that the economic transformation has been an entirely smooth process. Hong Kong, like any economy, is heterogeneous and multi-sectoral. Even though total unemployment has been low in the past decade, there might be significant worker displacement and structural unemployment in certain industries that may not be apparent in aggregation. Thus, an overall bill of health may obscure pockets of hardship experienced in certain sectors.

A hint of the potentially hidden problem is suggested by Table 4.1, which breaks down unemployed persons with a previous job by the industry of that job. The data reflect considerable variation across sectors. While the demand for labour in service industries has remained tight even in the last few years, other sectors, particularly manufacturing and construction, show a marked increase in unemployment after 1993. Not only are the rates of unemployment higher in the latter industries, but, in terms of numbers, they also contribute the most to the unemployed population.

The message from the data is not entirely clear, however, because these sectoral differences could be the result of either a cyclical downturn or of sectoral shifts. In fact, as is mentioned in the

Chapter 4

Table 4.1

Unemployed Persons who had a Previous Job by Previous Industry, 1988–96

Year	Manufacturing		Construction		Wholesale / Retail, Import / Export, Restaurants / Hotels		Services	
	No. ('000)	Rate (%)	No. ('000)	Rate (%)	No. ('000)	Rate (%)	No. ('000)	Rate (%)
1988	9.7	(1.09)	3.1	(1.30)	9.7	(1.43)	8.7	(0.94)
1989	8.0	(0.98)	2.0	(0.87)	9.6	(1.38)	5.8	(0.60)
1990	10.0	(1.29)	3.0	(1.30)	12.2	(1.69)	10.3	(1.04)
1991	13.1	(1.78)	4.7	(2.02)	15.1	(2.04)	12.7	(1.22)
1992	13.9	(2.12)	3.2	(1.35)	13.2	(1.71)	9.0	(0.85)
1993	14.8	(2.46)	3.6	(1.61)	14.7	(1.77)	11.5	(0.99)
1994	15.4	(2.70)	6.7	(2.85)	21.0	(2.45)	12.7	(1.00)
1995	28.5	(4.99)	14.4	(5.56)	27.4	(3.13)	22.1	(1.67)
1996	15.4	(3.23)	10.0	(3.48)	23.0	(2.49)	18.8	(1.40)

Source: Census and Statistics Department. *Quarterly Report on General Household Survey*, various issues.

Note: Figures are for the third quarter of each year and in thousand persons. The numbers in brackets are sectoral unemployment rates in percentage points, defined as: (no. of unemployed persons with previous job in the sector) ÷ (no. of unemployed persons with previous job in the sector + no. of persons engaged within the sector).

previous chapter, regression analysis using similar data up to 1993 reveals no significant relationship between sectoral unemployment and change in employment share. Whether the recent pattern is a temporary blip or a sign of worse problems to come remains to be seen. In any case, the sectors are still too broadly defined to provide any real insight at the micro level.

A clearer picture emerges if we take a closer look at more finely classified industries. Unemployment figures for these industries are available only since mid-1995, and they are shown in Table 4.2.

Table 4.2
Unemployment Rate by Detailed Industries, July–September 1996

Previous / Current Industry	Unemployed ('000)	Persons Engaged ('000)	Unemployment Rate (%)
Manufacturing	15.4	461.4	3.23
Food and beverage	0.4	21.0	1.87
Clothing and footwear	6.5	154.4	4.04
Paper and printing	2.5	61.8	3.89
Other manufacturing	6.0	224.5	2.60
Construction	10.0	227.0	3.48
Foundation / superstructure	6.7	195.7	3.31
Decoration / maintenance	3.2	81.3	3.79
Wholesale / retail, import / export, and restaurants / hotels	23.0	900.8	2.49
Wholesale / retail	9.2	367.2	2.44
Import / export trades	5.0	291.8	1.68
Restaurants / hotels	8.0	241.8	3.51
Transport, storage, and communications	6.6	334.3	1.94
Transport	5.9	288.7	2.00
Storage	0.2	3.6	5.26
Communications	0.5	42.0	1.18
Financing, insurance, real estate, and business services	5.9	351.6	1.65
Financing	1.2	117.3	1.01
Insurance	0.4	28.3	1.39
Real estate and business services	4.2	206.1	2.00
Community, social, and personal services	6.3	635.0	0.98
Public administration	0.4	124.4	0.32
Education, health, and welfare	2.0	243.4	0.81
Other services	3.9	267.2	1.44
Others	0.2	34.1	0.58

Source: Census and Statistics Department, *Quarterly Report on General Household Survey, July to September 1996*, Hong Kong: Government Printer, 1996.

There is higher within-sector than across-sector variation in unemployment rates, although these differences tend to be grossed over in aggregation. The relatively high unemployment rate in construction and in wholesale/retail and restaurants/hotels is perhaps more

Figure 4.1
Long-term Unemployment, 1986–96

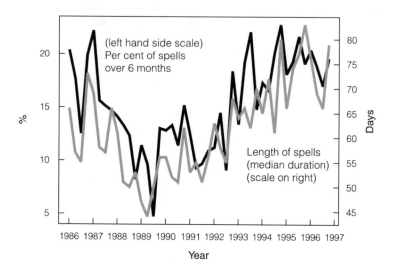

Source: Hong Kong Census and Statistics Department (various years).

cyclical in nature and may improve as the economy recovers. But the significant unemployment rate in manufacturing, particularly in clothing and footwear, which are export-oriented and hence are not affected as much by the recent slowdown in internal consumption, is likely to be related to diminished employment opportunities arising from economic restructuring and is therefore of a more permanent nature. While the published data series on detailed industries are still too short to clearly disentangle the secular and cyclical components, the high unemployment rate in some of the more narrowly defined industries that are known to be declining is a cause for concern.

More insight into this problem can be derived from Figure 4.1, which traces the time trend of long-term unemployment, defined as spells of more than six months, as a percentage of all unemployment spells since the mid-1980s (solid line). The initial dip is probably associated with strong secular growth that followed the take-off of the Chinese economy. Since mid-1989, however, there appears to have been an increasing prevalence of long-term unemployment, in synchrony with the accelerating restructuring of the Hong Kong economy, even when the overall labour market was very tight in the late 1980s and early 1990s. A similar trend is also exhibited by the increasing median duration of unemployment (dotted line).

One possible interpretation of these trends is that even though most unemployed workers have been able to find a new job within a reasonable period of time, thanks to a robust economy, there is an increasing number of workers who, having lost their jobs in the declining industries, are experiencing difficulties in finding satisfactory employment in either their initial sector or in another sector. And the longer they stay out of employment, the lower is their probability of finding new employment. The prospect for these workers is not good, since the lack of training for alternative employment, the erosion in confidence with prolonged idleness, and the stigma of long-term unemployment all work against them. These workers face uncertain futures and must often resort to welfare for maintenance. It is they who bear the brunt of the economic transformation and who are in gravest need of help.

Still, unemployment statistics do not tell the entire story. Apart from those job seekers who are not able to find employment, there are also some workers, included in the category of the economically inactive, who would otherwise have been in the labour force if sectoral shifts had not wiped out demand in many sectors. Among them are home-makers who would have sought re-entry into the labour market in their middle age. According to Mincer and Polachek (1974), women tend to have interrupted careers, drifting in and out of the labour market as their family obligations permit. But when their last child reaches school age, many of these by now middle-aged women would tend to seek employment on a more permanent basis. In the past, when the industrial structure was more stable over time, such re-entries would have been relatively easy, as these on-again, off-again home-makers would still retain some of the skills they acquired in their sporadic careers. But with the rapid economic restructuring that has occurred in the past decade or so, these women find that there are no market opportunities to "return" to, and they end up remaining as home-makers. Not counted as unemployed, this potentially large group of female workers simply disappears among the economically inactive in official statistics. The magnitude of this problem is suggested in a series of enquiries into labour mobility conducted by the government through the General Household Survey. The most recent results show that during the third quarter of 1995 there were 161,000 economically inactive persons who were willing to take up jobs if "suitable" employment were available. Of these, 117,000 (or 72.5%) were home-makers. This group amounted to 16.2% of all home-makers in Hong Kong. Even though these figures are compiled on the basis of responses to hypothetical questions rather than on the basis of concrete actions and are therefore relatively unreliable, and even though many respondents' concepts of "suitable employment" may be grossly unrealistic, the potential problem is of too large a scale to be ignored. At the very least, the phenomenon should be explored more deeply.

Even if they are able to find a job in one of the expanding industries, it is likely that displaced or re-entering workers who remain economically active will have to accept a substantial pay cut. Skills required in different sectors tend to be very different. Manufacturing workers will find that the human capital they accumulated through learning-by-doing in their previous job has little value in service industries that place a premium on interpersonal and communication skills. Age also becomes a factor, not only because learning becomes more difficult at a more advanced age but also because it reduces workers' incentive to acquire new sector-specific skills, as the period over which the returns from such an investment can be reaped before retirement is now shorter. Stuck with obsolete skills with little market value and little incentive to invest in new ones, workers would most likely have to settle for relatively low-paid, unskilled service jobs and a corresponding substantial reduction in living standard. They, too, are the casualties of economic progress, and the government is left with the difficult task of helping them re-establish themselves in the labour market.

Labour Shortage and the Increasing Demand for Skilled and Professional Workers

While sectoral shifts have left redundant labour in some sectors, robust secular growth in the economy has resulted in sustained tightness in the labour market in the past two decades. The situation is particularly acute in the expanding service sectors because of short-run mismatch in supply and demand. Only during the downturn of 1994–96 did we observe temporary relief, and even then the impact was different across sectors. This is illustrated in Table 4.3, which shows the vacancy rate by broad industrial groups in the past several years.

Two features are immediately apparent from the data in the table. First, the labour market was relatively tight in the early 1990s up until 1994, when vacancies started to fall with the onset of an economic downturn. The earlier tightness in the labour market fuelled calls for labour importation. Second, while the manufacturing vacancy rate dropped by two-thirds in less than six years, the reduction has been less pronounced in the service sectors, particularly in community, social, and personal services. The observation reflects the combined effect of both secular and cyclical factors. While both factors are simultaneously negative for declining industries like manufacturing, contributing to the drastic drop in vacancies, the cyclical contraction is partially offset by long-run expansion in the service industries, where labour demand remained relatively keen even during the recent downturn.

When considered by themselves, vacancy rates can, however, be very misleading. Like many statistics, they are sometimes interpreted without regard to the economic content of the underlying concept and are misused in public debate. Vacancy, like unemployment, is a function of wages, actual and expected. Workers become unemployed because actual wage offers fall short of their expectations, while employers fail to fill vacancies because the wages they offer do not meet the expectations of workers for the work involved. High vacancy rates may therefore simply reflect the fact

Table 4.3
Vacancy Rate by Industry, 1988–96
(%)

Year	Manuf.	Constr.	Elect / gas	Who / ret, imp / exp, rest / hot	Trans / storage / comm	Fin / ins / real est / busi serv	Com / soc / per services	All
	(1)	(2)	(3)	(4)	(5)	(6)	(7)	(8)
1988	6.12	9.42	1.63	4.69	3.38	4.01	3.37	4.82
1989	5.19	5.66	1.86	3.67	3.56	4.17	3.87	4.17
1990	4.72	2.56	1.80	3.55	2.69	3.24	3.25	3.77
1991	3.44	1.18	1.05	3.11	2.96	2.85	3.09	3.09
1992	3.24	0.85	0.86	3.42	2.66	2.86	3.30	3.15
1993	2.71	1.04	1.14	3.17	2.67	3.23	3.17	2.98
1994	2.68	1.59	0.97	3.19	2.66	3.29	3.50	3.06
1995	1.74	3.73	0.95	2.08	1.80	2.23	2.55	2.13
1996	1.76	2.11	0.20	1.88	1.98	1.76	2.65	2.56

Source: Census and Statistics Department, *Quarterly Report of Employment, Vacancies and Payroll Statistics*, various issues.

Note: Vacancy rate is defined as: (no. of vacancies) ÷ (no. of vacancies + no. of persons engaged). Figures are for September of each year and are expressed in percentage points. Abbreviations of the column headings are: (1) Manufacturing; (2) Construction; (3) Electricity and gas; (4) Wholesale / retail, import / export, restaurants / hotels; (5) Transportation, storage, communication and public utilities; (6) Finance, insurance, real estate, and business services; (7) Community, social, and personal services.

that expectations are temporarily lagging behind reality or that wages are being suppressed below market-clearing levels.

There are a number of reasons for why the latter possibility may be occurring. When the labour importation scheme was first introduced in the early 1990s quotas were set by the government according to a formula that includes vacancy rate as one of the considerations. There is therefore an incentive for employers to report high vacancies so as to enhance their chances of securing quotas. Indeed, during that period, unionists often complained about unreasonably low wages and about the high qualifications demanded from local applicants for certain jobs, which can be considered a demand-side analogy of "unemployed" home-makers professing to be available for immediate employment when the terms that they consider acceptable are quite impossible to meet in reality. Also, some firms may fail to offer market wages simply because they are no longer competitive in the face of international competition. Constrained by product prices set in the international market and faced with lower-cost alternatives in China, many operations, mostly manufacturing but also some services, are no longer viable in Hong Kong. High vacancy rates resulting from these situations must be distinguished from the commonly cited case of increasing demand in the face of an inelastic labour supply, which causes wage inflation. While intervention may be justified in the latter case, propping up declining industries or rewarding opportunistic employers (or encouraging such behaviour) are activities in which the government should not engage.

In order to form a more complete picture, recall the unemployment rates in Table 4.1, which show that, particularly in comparison with services, the manufacturing unemployment rate has been relatively high. This has been true not only in the past few years, when manufacturing vacancies showed a rapid drop, but also in the late 1980s and early 1990s, when manufacturing consistently reported the highest vacancy rates. These figures indicate that there is in fact a rather large pool of idle manufacturing workers who were not taking up the vacant positions in their former industries.

Part of the reason for the occurrence of this phenomenon may be found in Table 4.4, which gives the real wage indices by industries from 1988 to 1996. Despite the deceptively high vacancy rates and the persistent complaints of employers in the manufacturing industries about escalating labour costs, it can be seen that it is the service industries that have experienced the fastest wage growth. While the data from 1990 onward might have been tainted by the effects of labour importation programmes, manufacturing wage increases have lagged behind other sectors even in the late 1980s, when the manufacturing industries showed very high vacancy rates. Decomposing the data by broad occupational groups further shows that while wages of non-production workers in manufacturing have managed to largely keep pace with those of other industries, manufacturing craftsmen and operatives have experienced very little growth in real wages in the past eight years, and have, in fact, been suffering from a decline in recent years. This is all the more remarkable given the almost 30% increase in real wages for operatives in personal services over

Chapter 4

Table 4.4
Real Wage Indices by Industry, 1988–96

Year	Manuf.	Who / ret, imp / exp, rest / hot	Trans / storage / comm	Fin / ins / real est / busi serv	Com / soc / per services	All Industries
A. All workers						
1988	106.8	105.8	124.7	120.8	113.5	109.2
1989	108.7	108.9	133.8	130.6	126.1	112.4
1990	111.2	110.2	139.1	138.6	130.1	115.3
1991	110.0	108.9	141.6	137.6	125.4	114.2
1992	110.4	108.0	144.4	137.6	128.1	114.5
1993	112.5	110.4	148.3	143.1	131.0	117.2
1994	112.2	111.8	151.2	143.5	134.6	118.0
1995	108.9	110.2	148.3	142.8	133.7	116.3
1996	111.3	110.1	150.9	147.1	134.9	117.7
B. Supervisory, technical, clerical, and miscellaneous non-production workers						
1988	116.7	105.8	122.1	120.8	112.5	113.5
1989	121.1	108.9	132.7	130.6	125.2	118.7
1990	124.6	110.2	138.4	138.6	128.7	122.1
1991	123.9	108.9	141.7	137.6	121.9	121.1
1992	126.1	108.0	141.7	137.6	124.4	121.6
1993	130.1	110.4	145.9	143.1	127.1	124.8
1994	133.2	111.8	153.9	143.7	131.9	126.6
1995	130.9	110.2	153.6	143.0	130.4	125.2
1996	133.8	110.1	157.4	147.4	131.2	126.5
C. Craftsmen and operatives						
1988	103.7	n.a.	n.a.	n.a.	120.0	105.3
1989	104.9	n.a.	n.a.	n.a.	131.1	106.8
1990	107.2	n.a.	n.a.	n.a.	138.6	109.4
1991	105.7	n.a.	n.a.	n.a.	143.7	108.2
1992	105.6	n.a.	n.a.	n.a.	151.0	108.2
1993	106.8	n.a.	104.8	101.6	156.0	110.0
1994	104.5	n.a.	102.2	96.2	149.8	107.8
1995	100.6	n.a.	98.4	97.6	151.8	104.1
1996	103.0	n.a.	99.2	99.1	154.9	106.1

Source: Census and Statistics Department. *Monthly Digest of Statistics,* various issues.

Note: Figures refer to September of each year (March 1982 = 100). Abbreviations of column headings are the same as those in the Note of Table 4.3; n.a. means not available.

the same period. Whether stagnant wages for manufacturing production workers are the result of opportunistic behaviour of employers or, as is more likely, of cost constraints imposed by international competition, the picture of acute labour shortage and spiralling labour costs in manufacturing is an illusion.

This does not mean, however, that there has been no overall shortage of labour in Hong Kong in the past decade. After all Hong Kong's unemployment rate in the late 1980s and early 1990s was less than 2% — extremely low by any standard. It does imply that whatever shortage exists is concentrated among certain sectors and workers. In particular, the brain drain in the aftermath of the Sino-British agreement on the future of Hong Kong no doubt reduced the stock of better-educated and professional workers. The situation was alleviated by the economic downturn of 1994 and the concurrent wave of returnees among the many who had emigrated earlier, which swelled supply. But reverse migration will not continue indefinitely, and the economy is picking up again after two years of adjustment. With industrial restructuring also set to accelerate now that the reversion to Chinese sovereignty has taken place, and labour force participation expected to decrease at both ends of the age distribution, Hong Kong is poised for another round of resurgent demand for skilled workers. In short, while it must deal with the unemployment of many former manufacturing workers, the Hong Kong government also has to cope with the increasing labour demand that comes with the continued growth of the economy in general and of the service industries in particular.

Politicization of the Labour Market

Because of the short-run dislocation resulting from rapid economic transformation, there has been increasing pressure on the government to intervene in the labour market, to compensate "victims" for their losses, and to relieve difficulties that arise in the process. Employers press for effective ways of restraining wage inflation that they claim is weakening Hong Kong's competitiveness in

international markets, while workers and labour union leaders
demand better employment opportunities and resist any importation of labour that will increase competition. The Hong Kong government, more often than not, is caught in the middle of the political
tug of war and is being pulled in all directions by interest groups
who are intent on steering government policies in the direction that
benefits them.

Conflicting interests between business and labour have always
existed, and Hong Kong has seen more than its share of shocks that
have thrown the labour market and the general economy into temporary disequilibrium. In the past, though, the Hong Kong
government has been able to stand firmly on its general principle of
active non-intervention, keeping interference to a minimum and
allowing market forces to work and find the equilibrium. And work
they did, generally with admirable results, as is discussed in the previous chapter. However, the landscape of the political economy has
changed significantly in the past decade or so, and particularly in
the run-up to the resumption of Chinese sovereignty. Whether one
interprets it as a British conspiracy to undermine the administration
of Hong Kong in the post-colonial era, or as part of a logical and
irreversible development towards greater accountability and openness in government as the economy prospers and matures,
democratic reform in Hong Kong has brought grassroots representation into a political establishment long dominated by the
pro-business lobby. Not only are unions given additional seats in
the Legislative Council and greater representation in consultative
bodies, but political parties with strong grassroots support also
tend to dominate at the ballot box. With clear mandates from the
population, these politicians represent a force to be reckoned with,
and they have been vocal in promoting what they perceive to be
labour's interests. Very often, this brings to the fore the conflict
between the rising grassroots power and the entrenched, conservative business interests.

With fundamental changes in the political game, the government is finding it increasingly difficult to stay on the sidelines,
playing its role of impartial referee. As a result, the government is

now showing a greater propensity for resorting to administrative measures to satisfy special interests rather than relying on market mechanisms, and some of the policies that we have seen in recent years are promulgated more for political expediency than for economic efficiency. The suspended (but possibly soon to be revived) labour importation programme and the ongoing employees retraining programme, arguably the two most important initiatives in labour policy during this transitional period, are both examples of this phenomenon. Without going into detail about our prescriptions for these programmes, which we shall reserve for the next chapter, a brief history of the conception and evolution of the initiatives will highlight the way in which political interests have come to dominate the agenda for and dictate the outcome of what are basically economic policy issues.

The Labour Importation Programme

Because of the acute shortage of labour in certain industries documented earlier, the government, under intense pressure from the business sector, piloted a labour importation programme in 1989, allowing employers to recruit 3,000 workers from outside Hong Kong at the technician, craftsman, and supervisory levels on contracts not exceeding two years. This measure was subsequently expanded into the General Importation of Labour Scheme, which provided for the importation of a maximum of 25,000 workers. In addition, under the Special Scheme for Airport and Related Projects, contractors were allowed to bring in construction workers from overseas on the condition that the number of workers would not exceed 17,000 at any one time.

The business sector welcomed this policy, and after an initial lukewarm response due partly to the post-Tiananmen dip in economic confidence, applications have far exceeded available quotas in subsequent exercises. Labour unions, understandably incensed by what they saw as a blatant attempt at suppressing wages of local workers, objected vehemently. But if we take a more neutral stance and consider the merit of the scheme in terms of its impact on the welfare of the entire economy, then a case can perhaps be made for the policy. Labour services, just like any other services or commodities, can be traded, and it is natural that there will be mobility from economies in which the price (wage) of labour is low to economies in which it is high. Just as with any other commodity, such trade will bring benefits to both economies involved. So, if we uphold the principle of free trade, then labour mobility should not be restrained, either.

This argument is, of course, subject to serious qualifications. Any advanced economy will find that an uncontrolled influx of foreign workers and economic migrants can have grave social consequences, because workers, unlike other commodities, demand supporting social services and can claim privileges otherwise not available to them. This can cause resentment among the local population and discrimination against the imported workers. But perhaps the most important argument against labour importation is that, as with trade of any commodity, in the absence of appropriate compensation, not everyone will benefit, even though the entire economy will be better off. Some workers may find their wages lowered by the increased supply of labour even when the overall impact on the labour market is small.

While this localized wage effect cannot be completely avoided, its extent could have been more effectively controlled if the government had adopted an efficient method of allocation. Since the objective of the policy is to limit wage escalation due to labour shortage, the policy should have been targeted at sectors in which labour supply is inelastic and sharp wage increases are necessary to equilibrate the markets in the absence of additional workers. This could have been most efficiently achieved if the quotas had been auctioned off to highest bidders, as the bid reflects the value of the quota in terms of the savings in labour cost. By selling the quotas to firms that value them the most, not only could the government have ensured that the limited number of quotas — a scarce resource — would be efficiently allocated, but it could also have extracted the most revenue from the importers of labour to compensate local workers who are adversely affected by the policy, all at minimal administrative cost.

Unfortunately, government policies are not always adopted on the basis of efficiency. An auction strategy is, understandably, unpalatable to employers because all rents from labour importation would then be extracted by the government. In the end, the government came up with a politically acceptable formula that it claimed could objectively determine the optimum quota to be allocated to different industries. Since the quotas were given out free (apart from a levy to finance the employees retraining programme) to successful applicants, this method was favoured by employers. This attempt at replacing market mechanisms with administrative measures for the purpose of allocating resources (quotas) shared the fate of many similar efforts. In the initial years of the scheme, a significant percentage of quotas were reserved for declining manufacturing industries. Clear signs of miscalculation soon appeared, with under-subscription of manufacturing quotas and over-scription in the services. In later exercises, the quota system was significantly modified. But all discussions of the efficiency of the allocation mechanism became academic when, with the surge of unemployment in 1995–1996, the labour importation scheme was finally suspended under pressure from the labour sector.

In a recent turn of events, of which there have been many in the aftermath of the change of sovereignty, the government is apparently set on reviving the labour importation programme, a move the business sector is very much in favour of and labour unions are decidedly against. Recovery from the brief downturn and the decline in unemployment no doubt provides economic justification for the policy change. Firms in the construction sector, in particular, have been quick in coming up with forecasts of severe labour shortage in the face of the Chief Executive's ambitious plan to build 85,000 new residential units annually in the next few years, itself a project born of political pressure to lower property prices. However, one cannot but suspect that, whatever the inherent economic merits of the initiative may be, changes in the political makeup and in the orientation of the government might have been more instrumental in reviving its interest in the initiative than were any change in economic conditions. Whether the scheme will indeed be re-introduced, and whether the Special Administrative Region government will implement it with greater economic efficiency than its colonial predecessor did, remains to be seen.

Employees Retraining Programme

Until recently the government has played a limited role in the training of workers, primarily through statutory bodies like the Vocational Training Council. In 1992, however, the Employees Retraining Programme was launched, with the mission to retrain displaced and unemployed workers for employment in the changing economic environment. The Employees Retraining Board was established to co-ordinate the initiative, with funding from an injection from the government and a levy on employers in the labour importation scheme. Training services are provided by established training bodies whose course proposals are approved by the Board. The programme has since expanded significantly in scope as well as in coverage, with eligibility now extended to home-makers, the elderly, and the handicapped, and recently to new immigrants as well.

From the very beginning, the initiative has been trumpeted as the solution to the dual problems of unemployment and labour shortage that arise with structural transformation. If displaced manufacturing workers and home-makers can be retrained for employment in the expanding service industries, the government can, in effect, kill two birds with one stone. Ever the dismal science, however, economic theory suggests that this proposition is too good to be true. Quite unlike financing basic education, the benefits of retraining a worker are likely to accrue almost entirely to either the worker herself in terms of higher wages (because of enhanced skills), or to her future employer(s) in terms of lower wages (because of a larger supply of skilled workers) than otherwise, or to both.

External benefits to society at large are limited to secondary effects like lower welfare expenditures or less crime.

Therefore, if such training is worthwhile, i.e., if the benefits exceed the costs, then at least one party would have the incentive to pursue it even without government subsidy. The failure of many "displaced" workers or home-makers to promptly seek retraining and the general absence of private training initiatives targeted at these workers, either by employers on an on-the-job basis or by third-party vendors on a proprietary basis, seem to indicate that such activities do not pay off for these workers. If this is indeed the case, then the government would be investing in a socially inefficient project by funding these programmes, unless its involvement can result in efficiency gains over the private sector.

It is possible that some workers may be liquidity constrained: they lack the resources to pursue retraining even though it is worthwhile in the long run, and potential employers are unwilling to pay for it because of the absence of a guarantee that the workers, once trained, would remain employed. In this case, it can be argued that the government could improve social efficiency by lending workers the funds required for retraining. However, given the types of retraining that are provided, it is not obvious that the liquidity constraint is binding for many workers, even when time cost is figured into the calculation. Also, government financing of retraining does not require repayment, but instead offers fairly generous stipends (which have since been reduced) for trainees. This inevitably distorts incentives, invites abuses, and introduces offsetting inefficiencies.

However, in at least one sense, the retraining programme can be justified purely on efficiency grounds: if the importation of labour benefits the economy as a whole by reducing prices and inflation but hurts a certain segment of the labour force whose wages and employment opportunities are diminished, then redistribution of the social gains is necessary to achieve an outcome in which no one will be made worse off by the labour importation programme. Accordingly, the retraining programme can be seen as a means of compensating local workers for potential losses, and, despite official denial of any such link, the fact that retraining was partially financed by the levy on imported labour certainly seems to suggest that this was the underlying logic. Yet, from the way the two schemes are structured and targeted, it is not clear how much overlap there is between those who will be receiving retraining and those adversely affected by labour importation. The progressive expansion of coverage further accentuates the social welfare function of the initiative and makes an efficiency justification increasingly untenable.

Therefore, what was packaged and marketed as an efficient manpower policy can perhaps more appropriately be understood as a product of political expediency, a sweetener to make labour importation more palatable to local workers, and a redistributive instrument to benefit almost any disadvantaged group one could think of. Because the programme is trying to promise so much to so many, it is not surprising it ends up pleasing few. Some would argue that the programme is too generous and indiscriminate in its coverage; others would say it is inadequate and overly restrictive. Despite repeated claims of success by the government, surveys conducted by the Federation of Trade Unions and by the Hong Kong Catholic Committee on Labour Affairs have consistently revealed rather disappointing results on the post-training labour market performance of retrainees. While it would be fairer to say that the jury is still out on the effectiveness of the employees retraining programme, the problems that it faces are indicative of the difficulties inherent in designing and implementing sound policies when the government's very visible hand is increasingly being forced by political pressures.

Attempts at Wage Setting

Apart from trying to influence labour market policies, both business and labour have also often been less than subtle in their attempts to distort the market wage determination mechanism in order to seek redistribution in their favour. As is discussed in the previous chapter, wages in Hong Kong have been quite flexible, which helps equilibrate labour markets. As a result, the classic competitive labour market model basically applies, with few employers able to exercise monopsonistic power to exploit workers, and few unions able to force collective bargaining and wage concessions on employers. In such a market, each worker is paid her marginal revenue product, which reflects her productivity and the value of the output. While this is an efficient outcome, in the sense that it brings about efficient allocation of human resources to various production technology, or even a "fair" one (without going into precise definition of the criteria of fairness), it has not stopped either organized business or organized labour from pushing for "fairer" solutions which, predictably, are polar opposites of each other.

A number of regular surveys of wages and salaries in Hong Kong that are conducted by the government as well as by the private sector have sometimes been adopted as benchmarks for determining worker remuneration. In fact, the mere existence of such information, which is commonplace in most developed countries, together with overlapping ownership and interlocking directorship of some large corporations in Hong Kong, are sufficient to convince Turner and his colleagues (1980; 1991) that an implicit collusion exists among employers in wage determination. We are not ready to endorse such a verdict, not only because no hard evidence has been offered for what is basically an unprovable allegation, but also because the actual performance of the labour market in past decades, as is discussed in the last chapter, is not consistent with the non-competitive system depicted in those studies. Lately, however, not content with the purely informational role of these wage and salary statistics, business and employers associations have found it necessary to openly call for employers to confine pay raises to guideline percentages that are below inflation. Not to be outdone, rival labour unionists compete among themselves to come up with minimum acceptable wage raises that guarantee hefty real increases for all workers. Both sides present eloquent but spurious reasons for their proposals. Thus, the attempts to limit wage increases by business and employers associations are supposed to preserve the competitiveness of the Hong Kong economy, while the far larger wage increases sought by unions are supposed to ensure that workers can enjoy their legitimate shares of the fruits of economic progress. But the competitiveness of an economy lies in its ability to innovate and pursue its comparative advantage, and the contribution of a worker to the economy is already reflected in her market wage. Neither can be enhanced by artificially fixing the wage below or above the market-determined level. What one finds behind such rhetoric are simply efforts at rent redistribution through collusion and cartel formation which, ultimately, reduce efficiency and hamper the development of the overall economy.

Wage norms and wage controls have been tried by various governments, including those of Singapore and the United States, at times of high inflation, but they have usually proven ineffectual. In Hong Kong wage norms are not sanctioned by the government, and there have been few signs that the informal attempts that have been made have been successful in disrupting the market mechanism. As long as the economic structure remains intact and the interests within each camp remain diverse, market incentives will still prevail, and it is unlikely that any cartel, formal or informal, will have the cohesion and policing power to enforce any implicit or explicit collusion on wages.

Far more worrying, however, are legislative attempts at imposing collective bargaining. On the last day of the colonial legislative council, bypassing the normal consultation procedures in the legislative process, unionists and their allies successfully pushed through a number of labour laws, the most controversial of which commits employers of more than twenty workers to negotiate with labour unions on issues affecting employees' welfare if 15% or more of the workers are union members. Within days, at the behest of the Special Administrative Region government, which was opposed to these laws even in its previous existence, the laws were suspended by the newly established provisional legislature with equal efficiency. One may debate the legality and ethics of the strategies adopted by protagonists on both sides in their political manoeuvre, but the impact of such a law cannot be overemphasized. It would fundamentally change the basic mechanism of wage determination, with serious negative implications for the flexibility of the labour market and, ultimately, for the competitiveness of the economy and the welfare of the workers themselves. It is doubtful that the laws will be resurrected by the pro-business provisional legislature, at least in their current forms, but the government must remain vigilant against political decisions favouring either business or labour on issues that should be settled in the market, even in the face of increasing assertiveness of special interests on all sides. This is crucial if the new administration is to establish its credibility and commitment to a free and competitive economy.

Management of Human Resources — Matching Supply and Demand in the Longer Run

Since human capital is one of Hong Kong's most precious resources, it is important that it have a long-term investment strategy that ensures that its workers will receive the necessary education for the economy to remain competitive in the future. Unlike other commodities (or, for that matter, occupational training or retraining), optimal investment in education is not obtained in a free market, because individuals disregard the external benefits that their education will bring to society when they decide on how much to spend on education. Such an externality would result in under-investment in education, so that government intervention, in the form of subsidies or direct provision, is necessary to restore efficiency. But in order to allocate the appropriate amount of resources to different levels and types of education and training, governments often have to base their strategies on projections of supply and demand in the labour market.

The Hong Kong government's approach to forecasting manpower supply and requirements is conceptually simple though operationally cumbersome. On the supply side, natural changes and migration affect the size and demographic composition of the population, while labour force participation rates of the various age

Table 4.5
Projected and Actual Manpower Supply, 1996

Manpower Breakdown	Projection	By-Census	GHS
By Industry			
Manufacturing	540,100	574,867	514,400
Construction	243,200	245,440	280,100
Wholesale / retail, import / export, restaurants / hotels	922,300	757,239	887,100
Transport, storage, communications	312,300	330,974	344,800
Financing, insurance, real estate, business services	277,900	408,686	364,200
Community, social, and personal services	636,500	680,048	657,200
Others	42,500	46,444	33,300
Total	2,974,800	3,043,698	3,081,100
By Occupation			
Administrative and managerial workers	353,820	369,323	291,800
Professional, technical, and related workers	432,750	520,723	570,300
Clerical and related workers	542,490	512,719	555,700
Sales and service workers	790,170	419,721	428,100
Agricultural and fishery workers	20,620	23,478	10,000
Production and related workers	834,960	1,197,734	1,225,200
Total	2,974,800	3,043,698	3,081,100

Sources: Projected figures are from Education and Manpower Branch, *Manpower 2001 Revisited*. By-census and GHS figures are from Census and Statistics Department, *1996 By-Census, Summary Report*, and *Quarterly Report on General Household Survey, July to September 1996*, respectively.

Note: GHS=General Household Survey. Unit=persons.

and gender groups affect the size of the labour force. Once projections on changes in the key variables are made, and given assumptions of the government's educational policy, the future educational composition of the labour force can be predicted. On the demand side, given the educational requirements of different types of jobs, the projected changes in the occupational structure of each industry and the expected rate of restructuring of the industrial composition of the economy are taken into consideration in forecasting manpower requirements. Any difference between the projected educational composition of the labour force and the manpower requirements reflects imbalance that might have to be redressed through reallocation of educational and training resources.

Using this basic approach, the government published a number of manpower projections for the decade straddling the transition. The latest, which includes revisions based on data from the 1991 census (Education and Manpower Branch 1994), predicts a positive balance of workers at both ends of the education spectrum (form three or below and postgraduate level) by 1996, meaning that certain workers with the lowest educational attainment would not have the required education for the jobs they would be holding, while some with postgraduate degrees would be overqualified for their jobs. On the other hand, there is a sizable negative balance for those with an upper secondary and sixth form education, implying a shortage of workers at this level. The situation is going to be even more acute in 2001, with a widening shortfall in sixth formers and a larger surplus at the postgraduate level. While the report concludes that, overall, current manpower strategies are adequately preparing the population for future demands, the results also seem to call for some adjustments.

Before graduate students panic at their prospects and government planners rush to the drawing board, it should be pointed out that actual data so far have exposed a rather wide margin of error on these projections. Table 4.5 compares the projected figures for 1996 with actual data from the 1996 by-census and data from the General Household Survey for the second quarter of 1996. The manpower projection figures are based on 1991 census data as well as on the General Household Survey (GHS) and the Quarterly Survey of Employment and Vacancies (SEV), adjusted for mid-year. While the census and the GHS are household-based, the SEV is establishment-based and omits a number of sectors, including the civil service, many transport workers, and construction workers other than manual workers at construction sites. It therefore tends to present rather different estimates than do the other two surveys and is not included in the comparison.

It appears from Table 4.5 that there has been an overestimation of employment in wholesale/retail, import/export trades and in restaurants and hotels, while employment in services, particularly financing, insurance, real estate, and business services, has been grossly underestimated. As a result, the actual number of professionals and associate professionals exceeded expectations, while the number of sales and service workers fell far short. The increasingly strong demand for more and better-educated skilled professionals should lay rest to the fear that Hong Kong is over-educating its labour force.

To be sure, in any forecast, errors are inevitable. But the nature of manpower projection, at least in the case of Hong Kong, is subject to such exogenous uncertainty that accurate predictions become an all but impossible task. In projecting supply, fertility and mortality rates are relatively stable and predictable, but net immigration is far more volatile. There are, of course, strict policies on immigration, but the government has limited control over illegal immigration and virtually no control over the mobility of those with rights of abode in Hong Kong. Ultimately, the magnitude of these flows depend on economic and political conditions both here and abroad, which are highly unpredictable. As it turned out, the government's report assumed basically no gain in working-age population from immigration based on the belief that there would be a continued outflow in the run-up to 1997, when in fact there was a wave of net immigration in recent years, which added 154,000 persons to the Hong Kong population during 1992–94 (Suen 1995a). This no doubt contributed to the higher-than-expected aggregate employment level.

Similar problems beset the estimation of manpower requirements. Although economic integration with China and the ongoing process of structural transformation are set to continue after 1997, the actual rate is influenced by so many unpredictable and evolving factors, such as economic policies in China and cyclical fluctuations that impact different sectors differently, that coming up with an accurate estimate is extremely difficult. Table 4.5 clearly shows that the expansion of the service sector has been underestimated, while the cyclical contraction in retail, hotels, and restaurants employment surely could not have been anticipated.

Nor should they reasonably be expected to. Not in any forecast that is based only on linear projections. Not even in more sophisticated economic models that take into account wage and employment adjustments and therefore more adequately capture the essence of market behaviour. And surely not in Hong Kong. For on top of all the intrinsic imperfections in the methodology of forecasting, Hong Kong has always been, and is increasingly, internationalized, and consequently unpredictable. Hong Kong firms have been employing millions beyond its border, and hundreds of thousands of foreigners are making their living in the territory. The integration with the world economy in general and China in particular has blurred boundaries between the domestic and foreign labour markets, leaving local supply and demand more susceptible to exogenous shocks. Without the ability to predict these exogenous factors, any long-term, or even short-run manpower projections would be hopelessly imprecise.

This does not mean that manpower projections serve no purpose at all. However, we do believe that the key to the successful management of human resources does not lie in perfecting the art of crystal-ball gazing or in improving administrative control but in continuing the commitment to investing in the quality of our workers and in introducing enough flexibility into the education and training system. Currently the government is dominant in the provision, supervision, and financing of formal education as well as of vocational training, with private resources playing a basically secondary role. Such a centralized strategy relies heavily on the planning bureaucracy and does not encourage diversity. The recent proposal to impose Chinese as the language of instruction in all but a few select public and subsidized schools and the pledge of leaders of the Hong Kong Special Administrative Region to foster "patriotism" in schools raises the additional concern that the entire educational system will become even more of a monolithic establishment that lacks the diversity to satisfy, and the flexibility to respond promptly to, shifting demands in a fast evolving environment. If the government can introduce greater market incentives into the system and allow greater latitude for education and training providers, not only can the quality of service and customer satisfaction be more easily safeguarded in a more client-oriented system, but there will also be more innovations in education and training that can cater to the changing needs and aspirations of the population. Of course, the government will always have a financing role to ensure efficiency, a monitoring role to ensure the integrity and equity of the educational system, and indeed a planning role, because the delivery system takes time to build up. But a balance must be struck between the social principles behind centralized control and the allocative functions of market mechanisms. Indeed, the ability to achieve such a balance despite the vested interests within the establishment against a more open and decentralized system is an important element in maintaining the competitiveness of our labour force and the economic success of Hong Kong.

CHAPTER 5

Government Policies in a Dynamic Labour Market

Experience has taught us that, in general, resources are most efficiently allocated in a free and competitive market. This does not mean that the market solution is sacrosanct or that government interventions in market activities are necessarily detrimental to society. There are situations in which the free market fails to produce efficient results. An example is investment in education discussed in the previous chapter. Another caveat is that, "market failures" aside, economic efficiency is not the only criterion by which government policies are to be judged; political, social, and legal objectives are valid considerations as well. We do, however, believe that, in the absence of any market failure (or sometimes even in their presence), the government must have a very good reason for intervention to be justified. And even in cases in which other priorities take precedence, the government should try to formulate policies in a way that minimizes economic distortions. History is replete with examples of government measures that tried to suppress economic incentives. Such measures are generally self-defeating, resulting only in costly disruptions in the allocation of resources.

This is also the principle behind active non-intervention, the cornerstone of economic policies in Hong Kong. As one of the key links in the government's overall strategy, the design of labour market policies has also followed this principle. Nevertheless, because manpower policies have such a direct impact on the livelihood of so many workers, we have seen a disproportionate share of claims for exceptions to the rule, for government discretion in imposing arbitrary outcomes in the labour market. With pressure groups becoming increasingly sophisticated in these political exercises, it is all the more important that the basic principles be affirmed and consistently applied in assessing these demands for intervention.

Current labour market policies can be divided into two broad categories. First, there are policies which aim at maintaining a balance between the supply of and demand for workers in different markets. On the macroeconomic level, these policies, if optimally designed, can help to reduce adjustment costs and enhance stability in the process of economic growth. On the microeconomic level they can protect the interest of employers and the welfare of workers in the face of unanticipated shocks. The government's retraining initiative, labour importation, and long-term manpower strategy all fall into this category. Then there are policies that define the parameters within which the labour market operates. They are supposed to create a level playing field and to protect the rights of all workers. Examples are anti-discrimination laws and job security policies. Apart from these two major categories, there are also institutional mechanisms that help monitor the market and provide information on its performance so that timely remedial measures can be introduced where necessary. Procedures on collection and dissemination of various labour market statistics, particularly unemployment statistics, can have profound effects on public perceptions and government policies.

In this chapter we will explore each of these types of policies, their rationale, the available options and, where possible, the ways in which these options can be weighed on the basis of the principles discussed above. We do not attempt to offer definitive solutions, nor do we pretend that we know them, but by contributing our views and recommendations we hope to help set the agenda for a rational debate on the important labour policy issues at this crucial juncture in the development of Hong Kong's economy.

Government Policies Regulating the Demand and Supply of Workers

Training and Retraining Policies

The unemployment we experienced recently has both a cyclical and a structural component. The relatively quick recovery shows that the market mechanism is working, and that counter-cyclical policies are not really necessary to stabilize the economy. However, the increasing trend in long-term unemployment, particularly among manufacturing workers, points to a more persistent problem that calls for remedial measures on humanitarian if not efficiency grounds. Because many displaced workers lack marketable skills and the incentive to acquire them, government-financed retraining becomes an immediate and obvious solution to boost employment among them. Similar cases can be made for home-makers and other disadvantaged groups like the handicapped and the elderly, who are disadvantage in terms of their employment opportunities. New immigrants may have a strong incentive to invest, but they are likely to face liquidity constraints, particularly if they cannot work during the training period. Thus, coverage is extended to these groups.

Foreign Experience in Retraining

As is argued earlier, public investment in human capital along this line does not yield much in the way of external benefits for society beyond the private returns enjoyed by the trainees. Such investment is therefore likely to be inefficient because free or subsidized training distorts incentives and encourages overuse. Whether the programme in fact pays or not as a social investment is ultimately an empirical question that awaits a full evaluation; nevertheless, given the methodological difficulties inherent in such an exercise, the true answer, if there is one, may prove to be elusive. Foreign experiences in retraining have yielded perplexingly mixed results. See Ashenfelter (1978), Ashenfelter and Card (1985), Barsby (1972), Bloom

(1984, 1990), Kiefer (1979), LaLonde (1992), Leigh (1990), Orr et al. (1996), Gueron and Pauly (1991), Westat (1981), Bassi (1983), Bloom and McLaughlin (1982), Dickenson, Johnson, and West (1986), Geraci (1984), and Finifter (1987) for a small sample of the huge and growing literature. While it is understandable that programmes of different natures serving different populations in different periods would tend to produce diverse outcomes, different researchers using the same data can still come up with widely disparate conclusions. Barnow (1987), in a survey of a series of studies on U.S. training programmes funded under the Comprehensive Employment and Training Act, finds a wide range of estimates of programme impact on earnings and employment, from the significantly positive to the significantly negative. The main problem is that randomized experimental methods with scientific controls are usually infeasible in the evaluation of social programmes, while commonly adopted non-experimental approaches often involve arbitrariness in the selection of comparison groups, to which results are sensitive (LaLonde 1986; Fraker and Maynard 1987; LaLonde and Maynard 1987).

For this reason, it is obvious that we cannot look to foreign evaluation results for a clear recommendation on the retraining initiative. Given the hardship that many in the target groups experience due to factors beyond their control, society is probably willing to devote resources to retrain these workers even if it means, in the end, a certain degree of inefficiency. But in view of its intrinsic problems, it may not be wise for the government to oversell the programme as the cure-all that can simultaneously solve the manpower problem of the economy and restore the earning power of displaced workers. Doing so would only fuel unrealistic career expectations and result in frustration when they are not met, particularly since the government has a tough enough task simply in retraining workers who are generally of relatively low employability. Most retrainees are middle-aged, poorly educated, and probably of below-average labour force attachment and work incentives, and some have disabilities. All of these qualities make them harder to retrain and less competitive in the market even after being retrained. On the other hand, exactly because of the disadvantages of the target groups, the entire programme has to be designed to work efficiently so that public resources are not wasted on a routine effort to pacify pressure groups. Instead of blaming the workers for their failure to take advantage of the opportunities that the programme offers, we should set up a scheme that can maximize the retrainees' chance of success, given their attributes, while addressing the demands of the industries.

Unfortunately, the current strategy adopted by the government suffers from a number of limitations. For an initiative that is intended to match excess labour supply in certain sectors (including the household sector) to excess demand in others, the programme is making very little use of market signals and incentives in directing governmental resources. Apart from the fact that trainees basically face zero (or negative) cost in training and are therefore not encouraged to make prudent choices, the government is also relying heavily on the wisdom of administrators and training professionals who meet behind closed doors to decide what courses to finance. In other words, the training bodies are selling their proposed courses to the government when neither have specific ideas about the skills needed in the market. Input of those who know best, the employers, into course development is generally minimal. This separation of the buyer of the retraining services (the government) from the end-users of the product (the employers) means that, even with the best of intentions, the government is not in a position to ensure that the courses offered by the agencies it pays for actually satisfy the specific demand of the market. Indeed, a similar occupational targeting strategy adopted in a displaced worker retraining programme in Michigan has proved to be ineffective in improving the participants' re-employment prospects (Leigh 1990).

A More Efficient Retraining Strategy

It is therefore important that potential employers be more involved in the retraining effort, and at an early stage. Their involvement should be not only in terms of participation in planning committees (membership in which is inevitably restrictive), but also in the actual provision of training. In any case, courses offered by training bodies are necessarily generic in nature, and most trainees would have to go through considerable re-tuning by their employers, if they are lucky enough to find a job for which they are trained. From the employers' perspective, since they routinely have to train new employees anyway, they may be induced to provide the training at a lower cost than the training bodies would. Hence, on-the-job training is often more efficient than pre-employment training by third parties, and should be encouraged as an alternative to the conventional approach now favoured by the training establishment.

It is true that the Employees Retraining Board does finance some on-the-job training. Approved employers, mostly large firms invited by the Board to participate, can claim training allowances from the government for each eligible worker they hire without going through any prior screening by the government. Also, there are short-term wage subsidies for the employment of certain graduates of the retraining programme, which one can view as an allowance for on-the-job training. However, these initiatives remain limited in scope, and conventional skills training provided through training bodies is still the dominant strategy, both in terms of course offerings and of enrolment.

This is all the more puzzling given the fact that, based on foreign experience (and on local experience as well, by the Employees' Retraining Board's own admission), classroom teaching of skills has consistently shown lower cost effectiveness than other types of training such as on-the-job training and job search assistance (Bloom and Kulik 1986; Leigh 1990). The current model of full-time, intensive skills-training courses is favoured by training bodies, probably because they offer a stable source of funding for services that they are accustomed to providing. It is also favoured by unionists, perhaps because they find greater reassurance in the more substantial amount of resources involved. The trainees too, are attracted by the relatively generous stipend for these courses as well as by the promise of more "substantive" training and therefore higher-paid jobs upon graduation. But because there is no screening at the time of admission, it is quite probable that many trainees will be trained in skills that will not help them in their eventual career (if there is one), resulting in a waste of resources.

Given that many employers are interested in hiring workers with the right attitude, that they inclined to provide specific training rather than to rely on packaged courses provided by third-party vendors, we believe the retraining programme should focus on shorter, part-time courses on job-search and basic skills that aim at quickly helping the unemployed back on their feet. Once trainees are reconditioned to be more competitive, they can re-enter the labour market, and the government can offer wage incentives to encourage their employment. Greater effort should also be made to match workers with available jobs in the market. Even if intensive skills training is to be financed, stipends should be reduced or even eliminated. Most displaced or disadvantaged workers have a low opportunity cost of time, so stipends as compensation for the time cost of programme participation should be minimal. Immediate financial remunerations should not be tied to retraining, and those who cannot afford retraining should be subsidized through the welfare system instead. This way the government can redefine its role as facilitator and refocus its resources on cost-effective ways of helping those who can be helped. Throwing resources indiscriminately at all who care (or are induced) to seek help may convince the unemployed that the government has done its best and is therefore absolved from any further responsibilities, but it cannot be justified as a social investment, nor does it offer any consolation to those who fail to benefit.

Education Policies

One of the most important sources of economic growth and technological progress is the accumulation of human capital. Since there is a limit to the number of people that Hong Kong can support, education and training become the primary instrument through which Hong Kong can enhance its effective labour supply.

Since there is a tendency for the market to under-invest in education, the government must design optimum strategies to ensure efficient investment in different types of human capital.

However, the need for intervention does not necessarily imply government control. In Hong Kong the government not only finances but also sets the agenda for most aspects of the educational system, from curriculum to teachers' salaries, and from primary to tertiary education. With the exception of preschool education and a small number of international schools, there is no private market to speak of in formal education. This virtual monopoly by the government has the advantage of greater equality in educational opportunities. Yet the flip side of the coin is that the straitjacket of bureaucracy tends to limit alternatives and flexibility; it, too, tends to frustrate innovations in an industry in which constant renewal is the key to progress. The lack of alternatives also means that any miscalculation in policies will be propagated throughout the system, affecting entire generations of students. The almost complete absence of market incentives also deprives the system of any self-correction mechanism in the allocation of educational resources. While it would be unfair to dismiss wholesale the achievements of the government's educational policies, the fact that students these days often remind us of homogeneous assembly-line products certainly reflects the rigid educational and conformist environment in which they are nurtured.

This rigidity is also reflected in the highly hierarchical structure of the educational system. Early in their secondary school years, students are channelled progressively into different types of schooling and streams, with limited subsequent mobility. This tendency continues into tertiary education, with different institutions being competitors as much as complements of one another, each developing and zealously guarding its own specializations. The tragedy is that our future elites are spoonfed narrowly-focused programmes of study that are long on specialized knowledge but decidedly short on liberal arts education and language training. Such emphasis on streaming and specialization may be deeply rooted in the British tradition, but we are not at all convinced that it is the best strategy with which to foster a catholic outlook and versatility that is so important in a constantly changing domestic and international environment.

The English Language Issue

For all the faults of the colonial education system, the prominence of the use of English in schools has helped establish a strong bilingual culture that has laid the foundation for the success of Hong Kong as an international economic centre. Over the years, however, employers have reported a steady decline in language proficiency, both in Chinese and, particularly, in English. Instead of searching for a more effective approach to teaching languages and refocusing our educational priorities, the government is now proposing to switch to Chinese as the language of instruction in all subjects except English Language and English Literature. Only the few schools outside the public system, and certain schools within the system that can prove that they have the resources to continue teaching in English, are exempt. While this may be a politically-correct policy in the post-colonial era and will certainly please students (and, for that matter, many teachers) who would rather avoid as much as possible the frustrations in learning a foreign language, the new policy can have grave consequences for the future development of the economy as well as for the welfare of the students.

In the United States it has been suggested that bilingual education, which allows public schools in predominantly minority districts to teach in the students' native language (usually Spanish) might have hindered the assimilation of minorities into the social and economic mainstream, with detrimental effects on the subsequent economic performance of both the individual students and the ethnic group as a whole (Lazear 1995). This view is supported by McManus, Gould, and Welch (1983), who find that proficiency in English accounts for the entire differential in wages between Hispanics and whites in the United States.

The implication of these studies applies equally well to Hong Kong which is basically a small community within the world economic system where English (and to an increasing extent perhaps, Putonghua) is the dominant language. The de-emphasis of English in our society would raise transactions costs in our dealings with the external world and decrease our competitiveness. The potentially detrimental result is suggested in a recent study by Angrist and Lavy (1997). They analyze the effect of "Arabization" in Morocco, whereby French was replaced by Arabic as the language of instruction in the 1960s. The results show that there were substantial reductions in earnings and in the returns to schooling for young Moroccans, due primarily to a sharp reduction in French writing skills among students taught in Arabic instead of French. Apparently, whatever advantage there is in learning in the native language is not sufficient to compensate for the loss of proficiency in a language which has social significance and wider international currency. The evidence is all the more damning in that "Arabization" failed even to improve students' mathematical ability or their Arabic reading and writing skills. If the policy can have such a negative effect on a relatively closed economy like Morocco, the tremendous impact on Hong Kong, at a time when its position as an international financial centre is increasingly being challenged by other regional cities like Singapore, should not be underestimated.

Some may argue that use of Chinese as the language of instruction may improve economic and social ties with China, which may more than compensate for the losses in activities with other English-speaking economies. However, this argument ignores the fact that the proposed (or the de facto) dialect used in "Chinese" instruction is Cantonese rather than Putonghua, the official dialect in China, so that the policy cannot bring such offsetting benefits. Moreover, the current proposal does not offer any expansion of resources for language education. If the experience of Morocco is any guide, changing the language of instruction in Hong Kong will not necessarily improve students' proficiency in Chinese. It will only further stratify the educational system, with a minority of elite schools affirming their status at the top of the hierarchy by virtue of their English-teaching credentials, while language standard deteriorates further in "lesser" (at least in the eyes of parents) schools which cannot make the cut.

Instead of trying to "solve" the problem by avoiding it, we believe that language training, not just in English but also in Chinese (including spoken Putonghua), should be made a higher priority than it is right now. Literacy in both Chinese and English is important in order for Hong Kong to support a culturally diverse society and an open economy, and it must be maintained and strengthened if Hong Kong is to fulfill its destiny now that it has reverted to Chinese sovereignty. Skeptics would say that Hong Kong does not have enough qualified English (and, for that matter, Putonghua) teachers for continued emphasis on such a bi- (or multi-) lingual approach. The rebuttal comes from the success of some private international schools in Hong Kong where high standards of language education have been achieved for *both* languages. It may take a little longer and will certainly require more resources, but with determination, clear priorities, and an appropriate injection of market incentives, we believe the successful results of international schools can be replicated to a reasonable extent in the publicly financed system.

Market Incentives in the Educational System

The deficiency in language education is just one symptom of a more fundamental problem in the current public education system. With the government controlling all major initiatives, and schools and teachers finding greater security in the non-competitive environment, all innovations have to come from within the highly conservative bureaucratic establishment. Market forces are rarely allowed to play a role in the allocation of resources. When under-supplied factors such as good language teachers are not adequately remunerated, and when administrators are not rewarded for being innovative, it is no wonder that the school system is failing to keep pace with the development of society in producing citizens and workers of the calibre that we expect.

What we need is therefore not wiser directives from the Education Department on how language education or the entire system can be improved, but a breakup of the government's monopolistic grip on the educational system. The market should be allowed to do some of the work. The government must, of course, continue to subsidize education, but it should restrict its role to financing and loose monitoring to ensure integrity of the system; greater freedom should be given to school administrations in designing and delivering their services and to parents in their choice of schools for their children. This can be achieved through a simple change in the approach to financing education: instead of directly subsidizing schools, the government should instead subsidize parents for their children's education. This way, schools and teachers could no longer afford to be complacent, but would have to deliver quality education that is acceptable to the parents or else face elimination by competition. Schools would bid for the service of good teachers, and better pay would attract more qualified individuals to enter the profession. Successful schools would be rewarded financially with increased enrolment and could then expand their operation rather than being constrained by quotas imposed arbitrarily by the government. This would not only raise the overall quality of education but also encourage innovations and diversity. Different programmes will arise to satisfy different demands. To be sure, there would be a consolidation of the educational system in the short run as non-competitive schools and teachers would face the difficulty of shoring up their standards (as they should). Baselines and broad parameters would also have to be developed to ensure quality. But with proper guidance and assistance from the government, there is no reason why a smooth transition could not be achieved. In any case, the task that the government would have to face would be no more demanding than the all-controlling role that it is currently playing.

An International Centre for Higher Education

In Hong Kong, one area of education that the government has basically left to the free market is continuing education. With society becoming increasingly wealthy and the demand for skilled professionals becoming increasingly keen, many workers, including some who did not have the chance to receive tertiary education in the past when such opportunities were scarcer, have invested in upgrading their skills. In fact, the demand is so strong that not only local but also many foreign tertiary institutions have entered this lucrative market and now offer a wide range of part-time or distance learning programmes for mature students and working professionals. While local universities have generally been able to maintain a reasonable standard for their offerings, the quality of foreign ventures has been more variable. Since information about foreign institutions is often imperfect, some kind of accreditation or licensing standards may help protect local students from unscrupulous operations. Local institutions should also be encouraged to co-operate with foreign universities in developing new courses and programmes. Such arrangements can utilize the expertise of local institutions in finding reputable foreign partners and can enhance international recognition of the programmes as well as introduce students to a more cosmopolitan perspective.

The increasing internationalization of the market for higher education also demands a reconsideration of the role of our tertiary education institutions. The huge benefits that the United States reaps from its liberal subsidization of foreign students in American universities have far outstripped the costs that the it pays. In like manners, Hong Kong can be enriched by positioning its universities as regional centres of higher education. In particular, greater effort should be made to recruit, and more financial assistance should be offered to, mainland Chinese students. After graduation these students will help further the interests of Hong Kong whether they can stay in Hong Kong or not. Because of their special experience, many of those who move back to China should easily find employment with mainland branches or subsidiaries of Hong Kong firms and corporations. Even if they end up with no direct business connections with Hong Kong, the perspectives they acquire will, we hope, contribute to the further development and opening of China. Through whichever channel, such investment will pay off handsomely for Hong Kong in the long run.

Labour Importation Policies

As Hong Kong approached 1997, one of the most significant labour market trends has been the internationalization of its labour force. To some extent this is an inevitable outcome of the rise of Hong Kong as an economic powerhouse. People from all parts of the world flock to Hong Kong to work and to do business. Paradoxically, the internationalization of the workforce has also been a result of large number of people leaving the territory. According to government estimates, more than 600,000 people emigrated from Hong Kong in the 1980–95 period (Skeldon 1995; Hong Kong Government 1997). Some of them are staying in their host countries; some have returned. Those who are staying abroad now still have the right to come back to Hong Kong to work, and those who have returned can leave again at short notice. In the past decade fluctuations in labour supply have been dominated by emigration and return migration flows. This will remain so in the future. With many people who can legally choose to settle in Hong Kong or in another country, labour importation policies can only marginally affect the overall migration flows.

Foreign Professional Workers

Currently employment visas are granted to several categories of workers: professional and managerial workers, domestic helpers, and those who are admitted through various labour importation schemes. Hong Kong adopts a flexible policy towards admitting foreign skilled workers at the professional and managerial level. Their numbers have grown rapidly in recent years, from 12,000 in 1991 to 19,000 in 1996. Although these foreign professionals make up less than 1% of the labour force, they play a key role in maintaining the status of Hong Kong as an international centre for business and finance. In the past the Hong Kong government had given special favours to British nationals in appointments to civil service positions. This has generated some degree of resentment in certain segments of society. It is important to recognize, however, that the character of the foreign workforce in Hong Kong today is quite different from what it was twenty or thirty years ago. The proportion of foreigners working in the civil service has declined substantially, while more and more foreigners are working in the private sector. For example, the number of Britons in Hong Kong has grown by nearly 50% in the past decade (Skeldon 1995), even though the civil service has been pursuing a localization policy during this period. While the government may have discriminated against local Chinese in the past, the private sector can seldom afford such practices. The new crop of foreign workers are hired not for their nationality or for the colour of their skin, but for their contribution to output. They have brought expertise, connections, and new ideas into the territory, making Hong Kong an increasingly cosmopolitan city. Any change in policy to curb the entry of foreign professional and managerial workers or to impose localization of staff on the non-governmental sector will jeopardize the vitality and viability of Hong Kong as an international economic centre.

Importation of Less-skilled Labour

A more controversial policy issue is that of the importation of less-skilled workers into Hong Kong through the government's labour importation programme. The scheme has always been opposed by local trade unions, and it came under very heavy attacks when unemployment rose from 1.9% in 1994 to 3.2% in 1995. Reports of employer abuse (such as withholding wages entitled to the imported workers) also intensified the dissatisfaction with the scheme. Partly as a result of these criticisms, the government has decided to phase out the General Labour Importation Scheme and introduced a smaller-scale and more focused Supplementary Labour Importation Scheme.

As we show in Chapter 3, there is no evidence in Hong Kong or elsewhere that immigrants or imported workers will increase the rate of unemployment. In a separate analysis of the unemployment situation in 1995 Suen (1995a) argues that the major reason behind the rise in unemployment was a sudden increase in labour supply (mainly from return migrants) coupled with a slowdown in aggregate economic growth (especially in restaurants and the retail business). We dismiss labour importation as a significant factor explaining the rise in unemployment for several reasons. First, the number of workers brought in under various labour importation schemes is very small relative to the overall increase in the size of the labour force. In 1994 less than 5,000 workers were admitted under the General Labour Importation Scheme and the Special Scheme for Airport and Related Projects. In contrast, the labour force grew by nearly 100,000 people in that year. Second, the timing was not right. Fewer people entered Hong Kong under the labour importation schemes after 1992 than before 1992, and the government stopped issuing new quotas for imported workers in August 1994. Yet the unemployment rate did not begin to rise until the beginning of 1995. Third, imported workers are concentrated primarily near the lower end of the skills spectrum. However, people at all levels of skills experienced a rise in unemployment during that period. Thus, while labour importation might affect the opportunities of certain groups of local workers more than others, its overall impact on the labour market is small.

Although we question the view that labour importation contributes to increased unemployment, we do not endorse continued reliance on imported low-skill workers. Compared to a controlled immigration policy whereby accepted immigrants will gain full citizenship rights, a labour importation scheme has a number of drawbacks. As a transient group with no long-term future in Hong Kong, imported workers have little incentive to invest in human capital specific to the local job market. And by providing employers with a "quick fix" to labour market bottlenecks, the scheme also diminishes their incentive to offer training and to re-structure their business operations.

The economy of Hong Kong has shifted decidedly towards services and high value-added jobs. Chapter 3 shows that in the past decade wages for low-skill workers have not risen as fast as have wages for high-skill workers, and the degree of earnings inequality has increased. While allowing foreign professionals to work in Hong Kong will help quench the rising demand for skilled labour, importing low-skill workers will suppress wage growth for this group and widen wage inequality. It is ironic that the various labour importation schemes are geared towards workers at the lower end of the skills spectrum. The policy will only delay the much-needed upgrading in the human capital mix of the Hong Kong workforce.

There is also a social reason for curtailing importation of low-skill workers. Because their continued stay in Hong Kong is contingent on continued employment in the existing job, and because wages in Hong Kong are higher than in their home countries, imported workers can easily be held hostage by their employers. The threat of being fired carries a much higher penalty for imported workers than for other workers, and some employers do not shy away from abusing this power. The ill treatment of imported workers not only violates the law but also damages the state of employer-employee relations in general. Moreover, since imported workers are concentrated in some firms and industries, they form a particularly visible minority and can easily be targeted to feed anti-immigrant feelings. In some sense, the labour importation schemes have produced a designated group of "second class workers". Such development is conducive neither to harmonious labour relations nor to a harmonious social order.

For these reasons, labour importation policies should be adopted only under very special circumstances. The construction of the new airport is one such exceptional instance. The theory of investment suggests that as the scale of an investment project increases, the costs of adjustment will increase at an increasing rate (Nickell 1986). Thus a sudden and large increase in demand for construction workers would have to be accommodated by a disproportionately large increase in training and other costs associated with worker reallocation. The Alaskan Pipeline, for example, could not have been completed were it not for workers recruited from the lower forty-eight American states (Carrington 1996). Because the airport project in Hong Kong is known to be of limited duration, it will be very difficult to induce local workers to acquire the necessary project-related skills when they know full well that the demand for such skills will subside once the project is completed. If the government were to rely solely on local workers to

Table 5.1

**Estimated Number of Relatives of Hong Kong Residents Living in China, 1997
(Persons)**

	Spouses	Children
(1) Stock in 1991	95,000	310,000
(2) Entry into Hong Kong during 1991–96	102,000	112,000
(3) Estimated new additions to stock during 1991–96	26,000	32,000
(4) Estimated stock in 1997 [(1) – (2) + (3)]	19,000	230,000

Sources: Census and Statistics Department, *Social Data Collected by the General
          Household Survey: Special Topics Report No. VIII*, Hong Kong, Government
          Printer, 1993; and various issues of the *Hong Kong Annual Report*.
Note: New additions to stock during 1991–96 (row 3) are assumed to be equal to
          those in the 1986–91 period.

undertake such a massive public works project, the costs would
escalate sharply, the project would take much longer to finish, and
the many workers released on completion of the project would face
serious temporary problems in finding new jobs. We therefore
recommend that the General and the Supplementary Labour
Importation Schemes be considered separately from the Special
Scheme for Airport and Related Projects. The last scheme is an
entirely justifiable policy, but the former two should be phased out
gradually.

Immigration Policies

With natural changes in the indigenous population fairly
predictable, the wild card in the determination of population, and
therefore of labour supply, is net immigration. Hence immigration
policy, particularly in relation to China, plays an important role in
manpower policy for Hong Kong.

The Magnitude of the Immigration Problem

Hong Kong maintains a very strict quota for legal immigration
from China. Until 1994 this quota was kept at 75 people a day. It

was subsequently raised to 105 people and then further to 150 people per day. During the year 1996 about 61,000 Chinese immigrants came to settle in Hong Kong. Over 95% of them were the spouses or children of local residents (Hong Kong Government 1997).

The Chinese government controls who will be issued the "one-way permits" into Hong Kong; the Hong Kong government has no control over their issuance but controls the total number of these permits. Although most legal immigrants from China were issued permits for family reunification reasons, direct family members of Hong Kong citizens were not entitled as a matter of right to come to reside in Hong Kong before 1997. This situation has now changed. According to the Basic Law, Article 24(3), persons of Chinese nationality who are children of Hong Kong permanent residents have right of abode in the Hong Kong Special Administrative Region. However, persons who are wives or husbands of local residents but who live in China still do not have this right of residence.

Before the abolishment of the "touch base" policy in the early 1970s, immigrants from China were more likely to be men than women. As a result, the sex structure of the Hong Kong population is biased towards males in certain age groups. In 1991 the sex ratio among the 30–49 year-old ages group was 1,089 men to 1,000 women (Census and Statistics Department 1996). Many men in Hong Kong had wives and children in China before they arrived in the territory. Many others chose to go to China in search of a spouse. According to a special survey conducted in 1991 (Census and Statistics Department 1993b), 95,000 Hong Kong residents, of whom 93% were men, had spouses living in China. It was also estimated that 310,000 children of Hong Kong residents lived in China at the time of the survey. About 58% of these persons were aged below 30.

In Table 5.1 we use immigration records and some additional assumptions to estimate the number of these spouses and children of local residents expected to be living in China in the year 1997.

According to this update estimate, about 230,000 children of Hong Kong residents currently live in China. Not all such individuals will choose to settle in Hong Kong, especially those who already have a family in China. Some of these children do not have the right of abode in Hong Kong because their parents are not permanent Hong Kong residents. However, if we assume that everyone aged below 30 does have the right of abode and will exercise the right, the number of these newcomers to Hong Kong after 1997 will be about 134,000. Assuming further that they will enter Hong Kong over a period of two years, there will be a flow of about 67,000 persons a year. This is heavier than the current flow of 61,000 legal immigrants from China, but it is certainly far from a floodgate scenario.

A More Positive Response to Immigration

We are optimistic that the future flow of new immigrants will be beneficial to the local labour market in the long term. First, as we show in Chapter 2, the Hong Kong population structure is aging fast, and the fertility rate is extremely low. The proportion of the population aged below 15 fell from 23% in 1986 to 19% in 1996. Immigration would help to maintain a young and growing labour force, which is particularly important for providing income security to the elderly. Second, research indicates that immigration has very minimal adverse effects on the wages and employment of local workers. On the other hand, an additional supply of labour will help local employers. Third, many of these potential newcomers are quite young and will be exposed to the superior local education system. According to research conducted by Hon-Kwong Lui and Wing Suen (1996), immigrants who receive at least part of their education in Hong Kong enjoy a rate of return to schooling that is 2.4 percentage points higher than those who completed their education in China before arriving in Hong Kong. The younger immigrants therefore will stand a good chance of assimilating well into the labour market.

For all of the above reasons, the immigration policy in Hong Kong should not be built on fear. It is more important to assist legal

Chinese immigrants in their adaptation to Hong Kong than to resist the flow of immigrants altogether. The Education Department could do more to help immigrant children find schools. Special classes could be arranged to ease the transition to the new education system and to the use of Cantonese and English. For adults, the Labour Department could be a particularly useful resource, as immigrants know little about the local job market. The Employees Retraining Board may also extend more services to new immigrants, who will find such training most valuable. These additional services do not require a huge amount of resources. Helping immigrants help themselves can result in substantial payoffs to society.

Hong Kong is one of the very few places in the world where immigration of direct family members of local citizens is subject to stringent quotas. This has exacted a heavy toll on many cross-border families. Sad stories surface in the press every once in a while, but more often the anguish has to be endured silently day in and day out. Unfounded fear of immigration (and sometimes prejudice) has produced a callous indifference to the plight of these separated families. The Basic Law will redress some of these problems, but it does not go far enough. While foreign professional workers can bring their dependents into the territory, the spouses of local residents living in China still have no right to join their families in Hong Kong. While a local resident who marries a person in Singapore, say, can easily bring the spouse into Hong Kong, a resident who marries in China will face numerous problems in bringing the spouse home. It is time to change that. Table 5.1 suggests that there are only approximately 19,000 husbands and wives of local residents living in China in 1997, so their overall impact on Hong Kong will not be large. On the other hand, admitting them into Hong Kong will greatly reduce the number of single-parent families here, and the impact on children will be enormous. Cost-benefit calculations would therefore justify allowing the spouse of Hong Kong residents to settle in Hong Kong. In principle, people with husbands or wives in China deserve to be treated like everybody else. Why deny them the right to have a normal family life?

Legislative Initiatives

Equal Opportunity in Employment

There is little doubt that, on average, men earn more than women in the labour market. No one will disagree that the disabled face more problems in obtaining employment than able-bodied persons, that unemployment among elderly and young workers is higher than unemployment among prime age workers, and that British nationals in Hong Kong hold better jobs than most Filipinos. To what extent these systematic differences in labour market outcomes across groups are the result of labour market discrimination is less clear. The Hong Kong government has adopted a relatively cautious approach to taking legislative action against discri- mination. The Sex Discrimination Ordinance and the Disability Discrimination Ordinance were enacted in 1995 after more radical bills were defeated in the Legislative Council. The government is also undertaking studies on discrimination by family status, by sexual orientation, and by age. The Equal Opportunities Commission has been established for promoting equal opportunity and enforcing anti-discrimination in various areas including employment, education, the activities of clubs, and the activities of the government.

We will focus the discussion on equal opportunity in employment, but an example relating to education will illuminate the issues confronting equal-opportunity legislation. In Hong Kong some of the better government-run secondary schools are boys' schools. It is conceivable that the exclusion of girls from these schools could be subject to charges of discrimination. Refusal to admit girls into such schools will not be easy to justify in a court of law because decades of social science research has failed to come up with conclusive evidence that single-sex schools produce better students than do co-educational schools. We are not suggesting that boys' schools or girls' schools will become the target of anti-discrimination lawsuits; in fact single-sex school education is explicitly exempt from the provisions of the Sex Discrimination Ordinance. This is probably because many people do possess a tacit notion about the value of single-sex education. Tacit knowledge may not always be correct, but it is no less important than objective, verifiable knowledge. As Hayek (1945) points out, a successful economic organization relies on the effective use of tacit knowledge. However, because of the lack of verifiability, reasonable decisions based on tacit knowledge need not be defensible in a court of law. One danger of equal opportunity legislation is that it would promote the use of objective, quantifiable data at the expense of tacit, unverifiable knowledge.

Consider the question of equal opportunity in recruitment and in promotion, transfer, and training. In the *Code of Practice on Employment* under the Sex Discrimination Ordinance, the Equal Opportunities Commission recommends decisions to be made on the basis of "consistent selection criteria" and other measurable standards. These are criteria that are specifically related to the job, such as:

10.4.1 the type of experience the job holder should have, e.g., merchandising experience;

10.4.2 the amount of experience required for the job, e.g., five years experience;

10.4.3 the educational qualifications, if necessary, e.g., a diploma in merchandising;

10.4.4 the specific technical and managerial skills, e.g., use of certain computer software, proficiency in Cantonese and English;

10.4.5 the personal qualities required for the job, e.g., willingness to travel, willingness to meet people of different backgrounds; and

10.4.6 the physical and other skills required for the job, e.g., eye-hand co-ordination for delicate assembly work (Equal Opportunities Commission 1997, pp. 9–10).

Notable by their absence in this list are qualities such as general intelligence, ability and the willingness to learn, and attitude towards work. These attributes *can* be assessed (albeit imperfectly) upon personal interaction, but they are extremely difficult to be *communicated* to and *verified* by third parties. It would be a shame if employers had to forsake their good judgement in pursuit of personnel practices that are more defensible on an "objective" basis.

In a similar vein, numbers are much easier for outsiders to understand than subjective evaluations are. It is straightforward to show, for example, that appointments or promotions are disproportionately given to members of one sex in the statistical sense. It is much more difficult to show that appointments or promotions have been given to the most "suitable" candidates according to the employers' evaluations. By requiring decisions to be verifiably non-discriminatory, equal opportunity legislation can potentially lead to the use of implicit numerical quotas in employment decisions, hardly a "fair" outcome in a society that places great value on merit.

Even if an employer follows all the official equal opportunity guidelines to the letter, chances are that he or she would still have to exercise considerable discretion in making appointments or promotions. Should disputes be brought to the court, the question of which party should bear the burden of proving discrimination becomes important. Because of the lack of verifiability in employment relationships, it would be very costly in terms of record keeping for the employer to justify to the court every personnel decision he or she has made. In contrast, specific acts of discrimination are easier to document. A system that requires the employer to prove that discrimination did not exist would therefore entail much higher information cost than a system where the burden of proof is on the employees.

To conclude, no reasonable person would object to the basic principle of equal opportunity for all, but there is little agreement among people on what constitutes discrimination, or on the effectiveness of legislations in upholding the principle. Beset by intrinsic ambiguity in definition and problems in enforcement, government intervention may introduce more problems than solutions. Whether intervention is warranted should therefore be assessed by the social costs it raises, and by the extent of discrimination in the market in its absence. In the following sections, we shall analyze the issue as applied to different types of discrimination.

Sex Discrimination

Under the Sex Discrimination Ordinance it is unlawful to discriminate on the grounds of gender in the terms of employment or in the provision of benefits, facilities or services to employees. The Equal Opportunities Commission mandates the principle of "equal pay for equal work". That is, a female employee is entitled to equal employment benefits when she is doing "like work" or the same work as a man. Most Hong Kong employers follow this principle well before the enactment of the law, and the issue is relatively uncontroversial. However, in the *Code of Practice on Employment*, the Equal Opportunities Commission also "encourages" the progressive implementation of the principle of "equal pay for work of equal value". It is not clear what the legal status of the Commission's "encouragement" is, but "equal pay for work of equal value" is clearly a significant departure from the relatively uncontroversial principle of "equal work for equal pay".

The slogan that jobs of equal value warrant equal pay is deceptively simple. There is, however, a fatal flaw to this principle. The flaw stems from a fundamental misconception about the value of work. Value is inherently a subjective concept. In the absence of a market in which individual preferences are revealed, no amount of "objective" data is sufficient to determine whether an apple is more or less valuable than an orange. Similarly, in the absence of market-determined wages, no statistical procedure or job analysis will ever determine whether the work of an apple grower is more or less valuable than the work of an orange grower. If job values were compared "on the basis of the demands made on a worker in terms of effort, skill, responsibility and working conditions" (Equal Opportunities Commission 1997), then a philosopher would have every reason to envy a common street porter! An informationally efficient labour market (Hayek 1945) cannot afford to have wages set by these "objectively justifiable grounds". Taking the principle

Table 5.2

The Gender Earnings Gap across Countries

Country	Female–Male Earnings Ratio
Sweden	0.77
Australia	0.75
Norway	0.73
Austria	0.73
Hong Kong	**0.71**
Germany	0.69
United States	0.68
United Kingdom	0.63
Switzerland	0.62

Sources: Francine D. Blau and Lawrence M. Kahn (1992). "The Gender Earnings Gap:
Learning from International Comparisons," *American Economic Review* 82
(May): 533–538; Wing Suen (1995). "Gender Gap in Hong Kong: An
Update," *Asian Economic Journal* 9 (November): 311–319.

Note: Figure for Hong Kong is for the year 1991; figures for other countries are for
the mid–1980s.

of "equal pay for work of equal value" seriously will mean a fundamental change in the method of wage determination in Hong Kong.
We do not think the principle should in any way be encouraged.

Table 5.2 shows female–male earnings ratios in selected
developed countries. In 1991 Hong Kong had no sex discrimination
law. Yet in terms of the size of the gender earnings gap, Hong Kong
sits comfortably in a league of countries where various forms of
equal opportunity legislations were in place. In Chapter 3 we argue
that the increase in female earnings has been largely a result of the
rising labour force participation of women. Continued progress for
women will ultimately depend on their increasing attachment and
commitment to the labour force. A legislative approach may appeal
to those whose distaste for sexual discrimination demands a clear
legal statement (and penalty) against such offensive behaviour, but
it is unlikely to be as effective as market forces in promoting gender
neutrality in the work place.

Figure 5.1
Average Earnings of Hong Kong Residents by Place of Birth

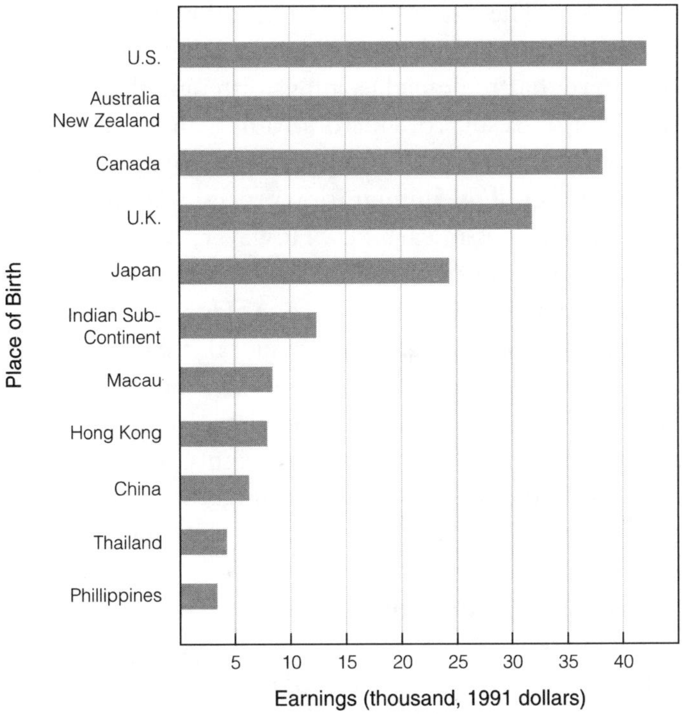

Source: Hong Kong Census and Statistics Department (various years).

Racial Discrimination

Racial discrimination is so sensitive an issue that the Hong Kong government has not put "equal opportunities by national origin" into the legislative agenda. Although Hong Kong is a fairly racially homogeneous city, about 5% of its population are not ethnic Chinese. Many of these foreign-born people occupy key positions in the political and economic system. At the same time, many non-Chinese residents are holding low-status jobs such as domestic helpers. Figure 5.1 shows the great disparity in average earnings across groups with different national origins. For example, the average Briton in Hong Kong earns about four times as much as a local-born worker, who in turn earns more than twice as much as a Filipino worker. The size of the earnings differentials across racial groups is an order of magnitude greater than that across the sexes.

We believe that the racial earnings differentials in Hong Kong are mainly the result of factors other than discrimination. Differences in human capital endowments across nations as well as the selection effect of the immigration process must account for the bulk of the disparities in earnings. However, we do not deny that racial discrimination does exist in certain segments of the labour market, particularly in the civil service. As Hong Kong was a British colony, the civil service gave preferential treatment to British nationals in appointment, in promotion, and in the terms of employment. This is beginning to change and will continue to change now that the reversion of sovereignty to China has taken place. For over a decade, the government has been pushing for staff localization in the civil service and in many semi-public organizations.

In some ways localization is a policy that has come too late. Twenty or thirty years ago localization of the civil service would have redressed some gross instances of racial discrimination. We do not expect, however, that discrimination against local Chinese will persist as the colonial influence in Hong Kong wanes. After 1997 a policy of localization is more likely to result in discrimination against non-Chinese workers than in equal opportunities for Chinese workers.

We do not believe that preferential treatment to local workers to undo past wrongs is morally or economically justified. For reasons of political expediency, it is understandable that top government officials in the Hong Kong Special Administrative Region should be Chinese nationals who are permanent residents of Hong Kong. In fact this requirement is stipulated in the Basic Law. Barring those top civil service positions, we see little reason to restrict the employment opportunities of non-ethnic Chinese. The localization policy, for example, has no place in a university, and it definitely should not be imposed on the private sector. As an international economic centre, employers in Hong Kong should always be encouraged to find the best-suited person for the job, regardless of his or her national origin.

Discrimination by Age and Disability

Unlike race and gender, age and physical or mental disability are intimately related to a person's productivity. It is difficult to sustain the view that skin colour will affect work productivity. It is not difficult at all (though it is politically incorrect) to maintain that people with learning disabilities are on average less productive than other workers.

Physiological changes over the life cycle imply definite changes in physical and mental strength. Individuals at different points of the life cycle also have different amounts of accumulated experience as well as different incentives to learn. These considerations suggest that it is unrealistic to assume that age is unrelated to productivity. In a detailed study of research publications in science, Stephan and Levin (1992) find evidence that scientists become less productive as they age. In another study using personnel data from one large company in the United States, Kotlikoff and Gokhale (1992) use a present-value model to estimate the age-productivity profile. They find that for each of the five occupation by sex groups considered, productivity falls with age, with productivity exceeding earnings when young and vice versa when old. For male office workers, for example, productivity rises initially with age until it peaks at age 45 and declines thereafter. The productivity at age 65 is less than one-third of peak productivity.

The Hong Kong government enacted a Disability Discrimination Ordinance in 1995 and is studying the possibility of age discrimination legislation. There is little evidence, however, that employers discriminate against these two groups, if by "discrimination" we mean unequal treatment based on *unfounded* evidence. Employers in Hong Kong, many of whom are not young, routinely give to charity causes that help the elderly and the disabled. The cynic might brush this aside as a corporate advertising expenditure. Yet respect for the old and concern for the disabled do seem to be a

Table 5.3
A Numerical Example of the Cost of Employment Stability

(1) Number of workers	(2) Revenue (high demand)	(3) Revenue (low demand)	(4) Labour cost	(5) Net revenue (high demand)	(6) Net revenue (low demand)
10	320	260	100	220	160
20	610	490	200	410	290
30	870	690	300	570	390
40	1100	860	400	700	460
50	1300	1000	500	800	500
60	1470	1110	600	870	**510**
70	1610	1190	700	910	490
80	1720	1240	800	**920**	440
90	1800	1260	900	900	360

Note: All figures are in thousand dollars per period. See text.

genuine part of the general public attitude in Hong Kong society. The reluctance to hire old or disabled workers in some jobs then appears to be more a matter of business calculations than a matter of bigotry. Education credentials, test scores, and years of experience are all useful but imperfect predictors of productivity. So are age and physical or mental conditions. Any one or any combination of these indicators will inevitably yield certain prediction errors. There is always a brilliant computer programmer who has not finished secondary school, or an energetic fifty-year old who still wants to learn something new every day. Employers will have to bear the costs of their mistakes, and they will balance these costs with the savings in information costs through the use of imperfect signals. A law that prohibits the use of imperfect signals is costly as well as arbitrary.

Job Security Policies

Employment security can be viewed at two different levels: at the level of the job or at the level of the economy as a whole. In Hong Kong, for example, overall employment has been fairly stable, even though manufacturing and other jobs were destroyed at a rapid rate. Whereas aggregate employment stability is widely held to be a desirable goal, the benefits from the security of individual jobs are less evident.

An Illustrative Example

Consider the following example of an employer facing fluctuating product demand. In the high-demand period, total revenue at different employment levels is shown in column (2) of Table 5.3, and column (3) shows revenue in the low-demand period. The assumed revenue structure reflects diminishing returns to labour: total revenue product increases at a decreasing rate as employment level rises. Assume the wage of a worker is $10,000 per period. Column (4) shows the total labour cost. Net revenue (total revenue less labour cost) in the high-demand period and in the low-demand period are shown in columns (5) and (6), respectively.

It is clear that the optimal strategy for the employer is to hire 80 workers in the high-demand period and to lay off 20 workers when demand is low. The average net revenue over the demand cycle will be 1/2($920,000 + $510,000) = $715,000. If the employer is prevented from shedding jobs when demand is slack, however, hiring eighty workers will only give an average net revenue of $680,000. The employer will do better to maintain a workforce of 70 people, with an average net revenue of $700,000. Notice that the policy of preserving jobs does not increase the average level of employment, while average net revenue is reduced. This conclusion is very general, and its validity does not depend on the specific numbers used in Table 5.3 for illustration. The optimal use of labour requires employment to be expanded in good times and to be contracted in bad times. Removing this flexibility in the employment decision will always result in lower average net revenues.

The above analysis is incomplete because we have ignored other costs of production. To give one example, suppose capital and other fixed costs amount to $710,000 per period. Then the employer would maintain a positive profit under the flexible employment regime but would not be able to survive under the stable employment regime. Instead of preserving jobs for some workers, the policy of job security would wipe out jobs for all workers in this firm! Even in less extreme situations the lower profits under an inflexible employment arrangement would tend to discourage business investments. In the long run this would hurt labour demand.

The International Experience

By mandating severance pay and a minimum notification period for the termination of employment, job security policies tend to raise labour adjustment costs. An increase in adjustment costs will reduce employment fluctuations *at the firm level*. (Theory does not predict how changes in adjustment costs will affect employment fluctuations at the aggregate level.) However, increasing adjustment costs also raise the full costs of labour. There is plenty of evidence that higher labour costs are associated with lower employment levels (Hamermesh 1993), though direct evidence on the effect of job security policies on aggregate employment is less conclusive. Based on a subjective ranking of job security policies in ten member countries of the Organisation for Economic Cooperation and Development, Bertola (1990) finds little relationship between job security policies and labour market outcomes. In another study, Edward Lazear (1990) uses data from 22 developed countries over 29 years to estimate the effects of state-mandated severance pay and minimum notification period on employment, unemployment, and labour force participation. He finds that "moving from no required severance pay to three months of required severance pay to employees with ten years of service would reduce the employment-population ratio by about 1 percent" (pp. 724–725).

In Hong Kong an employee who terminates the employment contract after ten years of continuous service is entitled to six and two-thirds (6.67) times his or her last month's salary (or a total of $150,000, whichever is less) in severance pay or long-service pay. While severance pay tends to increase labour costs, it is not uncommon for employers to offer such payment voluntarily in the employment contract. One function of severance pay is insurance. Another function is reduced labour turnover. As a form of deferred compensation, severance or long-service pay also helps guarantee work performance. For these reasons, and because our empirical knowledge about the effects of job security policies is still sketchy, we cannot reliably gauge the extent of the impact of government-mandated severance pay and long-service pay provisions on the Hong Kong labour market. We do know, however, that the level of mandated severance pay in Hong Kong is not low by international standard. In Lazear's (1990) data set of 22 developed countries, the average mandated severance pay in 1984 (the latest year in his study) was 4.9 months of salary upon dismissal after ten years of service, compared to 6.7 months in Hong Kong. The countries with higher mandated benefits than Hong Kong are Israel (8.4 months), Italy (15.9 months), and Spain (13.6 months). Hardly anyone would aspire to emulate the labour market performance of these three countries.

Unfair Dismissal

Another dimension of job security is protection against unfair dismissal. In Hong Kong the prevailing legal doctrine governing employment relationships is the at will contract. This common law doctrine maintains that employers are free "to discharge or retain employees at will for good cause or for no cause, or even for bad cause without thereby being guilty of an unlawful act *per se*" (Payne v. Western & Atlantic Railroad, 81 Tenn. 507 [1884]). At will employment is modified somewhat in Hong Kong by the provisions of the Employment Ordinance. Employers who summarily dismiss a worker have to pay wages in lieu of notice and to offer severance or long-service pay as specified by law, unless the dismissal is for reasons of employee malfeasance. Employers are also forbidden to dismiss workers for being pregnant or on sick leave, for participating in union activities, or for giving evidence to official enquiries in connection with the enforcement of the Employment Ordinance.

At Will Employment and its Exception

The utility of at will employment has to be understood in the context of pervasive uncertainty surrounding the employment relationship (Epstein 1984). In a typical employment contract, the nature of the labour service to be delivered cannot be fully specified in advance. Employees are expected to obey all reasonable orders from the employer. However, it is difficult for outside parties to determine whether orders are reasonable or whether a job has been performed satisfactorily. Both parties possess private information regarding the quality of the job, the quality of the worker, and the quality of the match. In these circumstances, an at will contract allows productive matches to be tried out while protecting the employer or employee from being stuck in a poor match. This strategy allows information to be revealed over time. Improved decisions can then be made on the basis of such new information.

Because the employment contract is incomplete, mechanisms to enforce contractual performance are also important. As in any exchange relationship, both the employer and the employee would expect to gain from a continued relationship if the match is an efficient one. The possibility of contract termination at will (i.e., discharge or resignation) then provides a self-enforcing mechanism that reduces the scope for opportunistic behaviour. MacLeod and Malcomson (1989), for example, have shown that any employment relationship that generates social surplus can be supported by an at will contract even though performance is not verifiable by the courts.

While the general principles of employment at will remain basically sound, many countries in Europe and in North America are gradually shifting away from this doctrine to varying degrees. In the United States, for example, three exception at will employment have evolved in different state courts. First, and most commonly, employers have been found liable for terminating employees who refused to violate a law or who exercised a statutorily protected right (the "public policy exception"). Second, some courts have held that terminations inconsistent with personnel handbooks, company manuals, or oral promises are a breach of the employment contract (the "implied contract exception"). Third, a small number of states have ruled that an implied covenant of fair dealing exists between the employer and the employee, and employees cannot be fired without cause (the "good faith exception"). An example of unfair dealing is an employer who fires an employee to avoid paying company pensions.

The Public Policy Exception

Dismissals based on capricious motives do occur, but they are not costless to employers. An employer who fires a valuable employee stands to lose some of the surplus from the employment relationship, and he will have to incur the costs arising from labour turnover. An employer who breaches the trust of workers by firing them before their deferred compensations are due stands to suffer a loss in reputation. The latter will be reflected in low morale among remaining employees as well as in high costs in finding new recruits. Furthermore, under existing Hong Kong law, unless the worker is summarily dismissed (which requires positive proof of misconduct), the employer has to give severance pay (to employees with at least two years of service) upon layoff, or long-service pay (to employees with at least five years of service) upon other dismissals. These considerations cannot completely prevent capricious dismissals, but they do make them relatively rare.

That unfair dismissals are relatively rare does not mean they are pardonable. Several public policy exceptions to employment at will are already in place in Hong Kong. For example, statutory protection from unfair dismissal is currently offered to workers who give evidence to authorities in connection with the enforcement of the Employment Ordinance or the Sex and Disability Discrimination Ordinances. We believe that such protection can be extended to a worker who supplies information to any official investigation. A general prohibition against the dismissal of workers who refuse to commit perjury or to carry out orders that violate the law, and a more rigorous enforcement of the existing provisions against firing workers for trade union activities, would also be welcome.

Implied Contract and Good Faith

Matters are more murky when it comes to dismissals involving the "implied contract exception" and the "good faith exception". Whereas public policy exceptions can be laid out relatively clearly, the determination of implied contract and good faith is expensive and prone to error. The costs arising from unfair dismissal lawsuits must then be balanced against the costs arising from the act of unfair dismissal itself. One enormous advantage of employment at will is that it is very cheap to administer. Any effort to use a for cause rule will allow a substantial fraction of dismissals (fair or unfair) to generate litigation. According to a study of 120 unjust dismissal cases that were decided by jury trial in the United States, Dertouzos, Holland, and Ebener (1988) find that the average legal fees exceed US$150,000 per case. And litigation expenses are just part of the story; the costs of judicial error cannot be ignored.

As we argue earlier, unfair dismissals do occur, but they are relatively rare. The vast majority of all dismissals are for legitimate business reasons. However, there are often cases where an employer fires an unsatisfactory worker who happens to be near pensionable age. Epstein (1984) mentions a case (Monge v. Beebe Rubber Co., 114 N. H. 130 [1974]) where a female employee refused to date the foreman eight months before she was dismissed. That employee also happened to have the lowest seniority at a time when work was slack. In short, attribution of motives is difficult, and mistakes are often made. A numerical example will illustrate the point.

Suppose out of 100 unfair dismissal cases, 10 cases involve genuine violation of implied contract or fair dealing. Let all cases of genuine unfair dismissal be correctly decided. However, no court system can avoid the possibility of incorrect conviction. Assume the probability of convicting an employer for unfair dismissal when he or she has not engaged in the practice is 20%. In statistical language, this amounts to saying that the probability of Type I error is 0 and the probability of Type II error is 0.2. Given the complexity of actual employment relationships and the difficulty of outsiders in attributing true motives, this is a fairly generous assumption regarding the accuracy of the courts. With these assumptions, we can expect to see 28 convictions (i.e., 10 + 90 × 0.2) for every 100 unfair dismissal cases. Of these 28 convictions, only 10 involve genuinely capricious motives; the remaining 18 are the result of judicial error. In other words, the probability of genuine unfair dismissal given conviction by the courts is less than one half.

A rational legal system has to balance the cost of incorrect conviction against the cost of undetected wrongful dismissal. If a productive worker is discharged unfairly, the cost to the worker is the fall in earnings following the discharge. If an unproductive worker is reinstated (or otherwise compensated) by the court as a result of judicial error, the cost to the firm is the difference between the worker's wage and his marginal product. These two types of costs are roughly of the same order of magnitude. However, three considerations speak against unfair dismissal legislation. First, a productive worker could probably find another good job after some searching, while an unproductive worker would like to stay in the same firm forever if given the chance. So, the cost of reinstating an unproductive worker will, in present value terms, exceed the cost of discharging a productive one. Second, as is shown in our numerical example, the number of incorrect convictions may exceed the number of genuine unfair dismissal cases. This result depends only on two assumptions, namely, that the fraction of truly capricious dismissals is small and that the probability of incorrect conviction is non-negligible. Third, the cost of the judicial process itself is enormous in comparison to a system of employment at will.

There are relatively few empirical studies of the actual effects of unfair dismissal laws. In a time series study of unemployment in Britain for the period from 1967 to 1977, Stephen Nickell (1982) finds that an increase in the number of unfair dismissal cases causes both a reduction in hiring and a reduction in job separations. The latter effect dominates so that the number of unfair dismissal cases is negatively related to the unemployment rate. In another study, Dertouzos and Karoly (1993) use 1980 to 1987 state-level data in the United States describing employment outcomes and state court doctrines concerning unfair dismissal. They find that following the tort versions of the good faith exceptions to employment at will results in a significant reduction in employment level. At this stage, evidence on the effect of unfair dismissal laws on employment is therefore still inconclusive. As long as dismissals by reasons of redundancy are held to be legal *per se*, we believe that any effect on the *aggregate* level of employment or unemployment is probably minor. By making firing more difficult, however, unfair dismissal laws will tend to reduce efficient labour turnover. Moreover, the high administrative costs and the potential costs from incorrect judicial decisions are very likely to be greater than the costs arising from unjust dismissals. Whereas a public policy exception to employment at will can be supported because it is reasonably clear and because the integrity of public policies is at stake, a broad unfair dismissal law is not justifiable on cost–benefit grounds.

The Politics of Unemployment Statistics and the Administrative Control of Information

In economics, the conceptual distinction between the unemployed and the economically inactive has never been very clearly defined. Individuals without a job and not looking for one will sometimes be tempted to take up market employment if the opportunity is good enough, while others, the "discouraged workers", simply give up looking because they do not perceive that employment is available. Even though these people are willing to work if an appropriate job can be found, and are therefore not much different from the officially unemployed, they are often not counted as unemployed, because in many countries, to qualify as such, they would have to be actively searching for a job.

Nor does international convention provide very clear guidelines for precise definitions of the concepts. In 1982 the Thirteenth International Conference of Labour Statisticians passed a "resolution concerning statistics of the economically active population, employment, unemployment and underemployment". On the concept of unemployment, it is resolved that:

1. The "unemployed" comprise all persons above a specified age who during the reference period were:
   a) "without work", i.e., were not in paid employment or self-employment . . . ;
   b) "currently available for work", i.e., were available for paid employment or self-employment during the reference period; and
   c) "seeking work", i.e., had taken specific steps in a specified recent period to seek paid employment or self-employment. Such specific steps may include registration at a public or private employment exchange; application to employers; checking work-sites, farms, factory gates, markets, or other assembly places; placing or answering newspaper advertisements; asking assistance of friends or relatives; looking for land, building, machinery or equipment to establish own enterprise; arranging for financial resources; applying for permits and licenses (International Labour Office 1983, XII).

These guidelines would have provided for a very clear operational definition for unemployment, but then the resolution proceeds to qualify that:

2. In situations where the conventional means of seeking work are of limited relevance, where the labour market is largely unorganized or of limited scope, where labour absorption is, at the time, inadequate, or where the labour force is largely self-employed, the standard definition of unemployment . . . may be applied by relaxing the criterion of seeking work.
3. In the application of the criterion of current availability for work, . . . appropriate tests should be developed to suit national circumstances. Such tests may be based on

Table 5.4

Official and Trade Union Estimates of Unemployment Rates

(%)

	94Q4	95Q1	95Q2	95Q3	95Q4	96Q1	96Q2	96Q3	96Q4
Official estimates	1.9	2.6	2.9	3.7	3.5	3.0	2.9	2.6	2.7
Trade union estimates	7.1	9.5	12.1	13.1	9.0	10.5	8.4	9.4	11.3

Note: Figures are in percentage points. Official estimates are based on the General Household Survey conducted by the Census and Statistics Department. Trade union estimates are based on surveys conducted by the Federation of Trade Unions. 94Q4 means the 4th quarter of 1994.

notions such as present desire for work and previous work experience, willingness to take work for wage or salary on locally prevailing terms, or readiness to undertake self-employment activity given the necessary resources and facilities.

4.   . . . [P]ersons without work and currently available for work who had made arrangement to take up paid employment or undertake self-employment activity at a date subsequent to the reference period should be considered unemployed.

5. Persons temporarily absent from their jobs with no formal job attachment who were currently available for work and seeking work should be regarded as unemployed . . .

6. Students, homemakers and others mainly engaged in economic activities during the reference period who satisfy the criteria laid down in sub-paragraphs (1) and (2) above should be regarded as unemployed . . . (International Labour Office 1983).

Items (2) and (3) above, in particular, introduce such latitude in the criteria of seeking work and availability for work that almost any definition of unemployment can be accommodated. With such a wide margin between the most inclusive and exclusive criteria, the measurement of unemployment is, at best, a rather arbitrary exercise.

Controversy over Unemployment Statistics

Because of the ambiguity in the definition of unemployment, and because of its potentially significant policy implications, the debate over what constitutes unemployment and how it should be measured can take on strong political overtones. In Hong Kong this issue was brought to the fore in a recent row in which the Federation of Trade Unions (FTU) accused the government of under-reporting unemployment in order to sweep the unemployment problem under the rug. Long suspicious of what it considers to be unrealistically low unemployment figures, the FTU started to survey its own members and compile an alternative unemployment rate in 1995. As expected, the results, as shown in Table 5.4, give far higher estimates, exceeding the official rates by two to three times.

The controversy was further fuelled by a recent special report on labour mobility (Census and Statistics Department 1997), which found that, during September to October of 1995, there were 161,000 economically inactive individuals who were willing to take up jobs if "suitable employment" were available. The majority of them (72.5%) were housewives. The FTU believed that this large population of individuals were conceptually indistinguishable from the discouraged workers and should be considered unemployed. The fact that they were not further convinced the FTU of a government conspiracy to cover up the extent of the unemployment problem.

It is to be expected that social activists and pressure groups are generally cynical about information disseminated by the government. It is also true that suspected conspiracies would often be less sensationally interpreted if evidence were more objectively weighted. Indeed, much of the difference between government and FTU statistics can be attributed to differences in sampling and survey methodologies.

The government uses data from the General Household Survey (GHS) for compiling unemployment statistics. The GHS is a quarterly survey of a sample of households that are representative of the land-based, civilian, non-institutional population in Hong Kong. In the second quarter of 1996, 23,000 households were sampled, which represent approximately 1.25% of all households. Given an average household size of 3.3 persons and taking out the 18.5% who are below age 15, the sample amounts to around 63,000 working-age persons. About half of the selected quarters are visited personally by interviewers; the rest of the residents are interviewed by telephone. On the other hand, the quarterly survey conducted by the FTU randomly selects a much smaller sample of 2,000 to 3,000 individuals from among its membership of around 200,000 for telephone interviews. As members of the FTU are generally less educated, older, and over-represented in the declining industries compared to the general labour force, it is not surprising that they tend to show higher unemployment. The more resourceful efforts made by the Census and Statistics Department in reaching the selected households also make a significant difference. Instead of relying exclusively on telephone contacts, more aggressive follow-ups including repeated in-person visits have consistently resulted in a success rate of more than 95% in GHS surveys. In comparison, the FTU has been able to reach only around 40% of those enumerated in each survey. Such a low success rate will surely introduce an upward bias in estimated unemployment, as employed individuals are less likely to be home and are therefore under-represented among the telephone interviewees.

Even though both surveys ask similar questions in ascertaining the labour market status of the subjects, they differ in details and in interpretations. Apparently, in the FTU survey, any worker not seeking work because she believes there are no "suitable" jobs in the market for her or because she believes pay is too low for the available jobs is automatically counted as a discouraged worker and is therefore considered unemployed. The government survey, on the other hand, imposes stricter standards based on the subject's "present desire for work ... and willingness to take work for wage or salary on locally prevailing terms", in accordance with the International Labour Office resolution. Interviewees are prompted for what they consider to be suitable employment or reasonable pay in determining whether they are realistic in their expectations. This would screen out from the ranks of the unemployed certain workers whose job aspirations are not likely to be met under the prevailing market conditions.

Incidentally, this difference in the definition of a discouraged worker may also account for most of the 117,000 home-makers who claim to be willing to take up employment in the government's labour mobility report cited by the FTU. According to the Census and Statistics Department, most of these subjects are full-time housewives who initially responded that they were not available for employment (presumably because of family obligations) or whose manifested expectations for wages or flexibility in working hours are unrealistic. As the report emphasizes, the questions asked in the special survey were hypothetical, and the subjects' professed willingness to work cannot always be taken at face value without consideration of the conditions that go with such willingness. For this reason, although the ambiguity in the concept dictates that the government might have wrongly determined the status of some of the home-makers in the report, the FTU's claim that all of them are discouraged workers whose eagerness to work is frustrated only by discrimination or lack of opportunities seems more than a little inflated.

So, which figures are more "accurate"? Given the unavoidable arbitrariness in this political number game, there are no absolutely "correct" unemployment statistics. Because of the restrictiveness of the FTU samples, the union's reported statistics should be interpreted as reflecting the experience of a more special class of grassroots workers rather than of the population as a whole. Given that the target group tends to be more adversely affected by the economic transformation of Hong Kong, such a survey would help focus on their plight, but even then the FTU might have to modify its survey methodology to remove the potential biases inherent in its current strategy.

The official figures published by the Hong Kong government are not flawless either, but they are not any more flawed than those published by most other countries. Nor are there any market peculiarities or government policies that tend to hide unemployment behind retraining or other non-productive activities, as is the case in some Scandinavian countries and in Japan. In fact, given that discouraged workers are included among the unemployed in Hong Kong while they are not in such countries as the United States, Hong Kong's official statistics are already slightly inflated by comparison.

Towards Greater Openness in the Use of Data

Even if we are satisfied that the government's approach falls well within international guidelines, we do believe that the Census and Statistics Department should take more seriously its responsibility of publicizing its methodology and findings. Information on social and economic indicators are of more than academic interests to the public, and much misunderstanding by the public could have been avoided if the government had made the effort to better explain its statistics in the first place rather than to wait for inquiries.

The recent controversy between the FTU and the government reflects a more general problem in the operation of the Census and Statistics Department. Data tend to be jealously guarded, and the public is generally expected to be satisfied with whatever information is published in official reports, which are sometimes under-documented. While published statistics can be quite detailed, they are usually in tabulated form and are often inadequate for in-depth analysis in independent research. Procedures for the use of raw survey data files are restrictive and do much to discourage access. It is certainly true that the government must protect the confidentiality of survey respondents, but other countries with strict privacy laws, including the United States, have long had in place procedures that can achieve this without undue barriers to access. This general lack of transparency may facilitate bureaucratic control, but it allows the government to monopolize information and is hardly in step with the general trend towards greater openness in government. Surely a better balance can be struck, and it is perhaps time that the Department re-evaluates its procedures.

CHAPTER 6

Conclusion

Few people would fail to be amazed by the rags to riches story of Hong Kong. In less than one and a half century, it has transformed itself from a small fishing village to a modern, international financial centre. The people of Hong Kong, once impoverished and consisted mostly of refugees, now enjoy an income level which is among the highest in the world, surpassing even many developed western economies. This story is all the more remarkable because the success has been achieved largely without government intervention, and the case of Hong Kong now serves as a living testimony of the power of the free market.

The success of the Hong Kong economy is mirrored in the generally smooth performance of its labour market. Hong Kong has absorbed wave after wave of refugees and immigrants and survived episodes of brain drain resulting from confidence crises, global recessions, and rapid structural transformation of the economy. Yet it has not suffered from the chronic unemployment problems that have been plaguing many other countries. This is because, unlike other economies where workers are "protected" from the vicissitudes of the market, wages are flexible and workers are mobile in Hong Kong. Flexibility and mobility help equilibrate the markets and avoid prolonged periods of dislocation. The smooth performance should also lay to rest the belief held by some (Turner 1980; Chau 1993) that, in Hong Kong, real wages do not adjust quickly to reflect market conditions, and that workers are incapable of deriving correct information from market signals, so that government assistance is necessary to ensure efficiency. That the market works is not a statement of faith; it is a hypothesis substantiated by empirical experience.

Nor are the benefits of economic progress restricted to a select few. By and large, most people have enjoyed a substantial improvement in living standards over the years. The recent increase in income inequality is more the result of larger gains by high income individuals rather than of a worsening of conditions of the poor. Nevertheless, it is true that some workers might have lagged behind others, having been adversely affected by the economic restructuring, and that new immigrants have to face the problems of integrating into society. Older generations have gone through similar problems before, but since our priorities do change over time as society progresses, it is reasonable to expect the government to do more than it did in the past in relieving the hardship of these people. However, these efforts should be taken within the parameters of the existing system. Any fundamental change that distorts Hong Kong's basic economic principles will have detrimental effects in the long run.

In this spirit, therefore, we are opposed to a legislative approach to enhance worker welfare and promote equality in the labour market. There is always a tendency to attribute observed differences in labour market experience between groups of workers to discrimination that should be banned by introducing new laws. This is a well-meaning but very simplistic solution to a perception that is based on a superficial interpretation of the observations. The Legislative appeal is that it is direct and simplistic. It must be pointed out that, in a labour market as competitive as Hong Kong's, apparent incidents of discrimination are often results of rational economic decisions by employers and workers. While there are genuine cases of discrimination, the intrinsic difficulty in distinguishing them from predominately legitimate decisions makes legislation an inappropriate prescription for a delicate problem. Similarly, legislations that appear to guarantee more benefits for workers only serve to limit flexibility of firms in offering compensation packages that appeal to workers with different preferences, and to increase the fixed cost of employment. In the long run it is the workers, and indeed the entire economy, that will be hurt by the resulting inefficiency, a paradox apparently lost on crusaders for worker rights.

This, then, is not the time to tamper with the system that has made Hong Kong the miracle it is. As long as the basic tenets of the system remain intact, we believe the Hong Kong economy and the labour market will continue to be as resilient and vibrant as they have been in the past, capable of meeting the challenges that await us in the new millennium. Unlike those who try to trace economic success to cultural, racial, or national characteristics, we believe market forces are universal. If the change of sovereignty does not alter the basic incentives or pervert the structure of the free market system, then there is no reason that the economic miracle born under British rule cannot continue now that Hong Kong has re-established its Chinese lineage. But this does not mean that the road ahead will be smooth. Reversion to Chinese sovereignty is bound to magnify some of the problems that we are experiencing. The closer economic relation between Hong Kong and China will accelerate Hong Kong's structural transformation. Such a trend will not bode well to workers who have lost their jobs to sectoral shifts, or to many others whose employment will be threatened. Moreover, the expected increase in immigration from China, legal or otherwise, will increase competition for lower-skilled jobs, depress wages, and increase income inequality. In the end, the workers' own initiative will determine their futures. Nevertheless, the government should also be prepared to offer help, in a focused effort, through short-term retraining or assistance in job matching, so that at least some displaced workers will be able to re-establish themselves in the labour market.

With the expansion of the service industries set to continue, shortage of labour in those sectors will remain a problem. At present, targeted immigration based on professional skills is apparently not on the government's agenda, so endogenous adjustment in supply is the only viable solution in the long run. If our educational and training system is flexible, then market incentives will ensure that, given time, workers will enter sectors where there are excess demands, and equilibrium will be restored. As adjustments will take time, the situation is more uncertain in the short run. Already the government has indicated interest in reviving the suspended labour importation programme. Considering the approach adopted in earlier exercises, we are doubtful that such an initiative can effectively tackle the problem of labour shortage, and that it is worth the social cost. Even if the government proceeds with labour importation, it should at least re-think the strategy so that the additional resources can be more efficiently allocated.

Ultimately, however, economic activities in a society that prides itself on the rule of law must operate within constraints that are set politically, although over time, these constraints are in turn influenced by economic forces. The uncertainty over the political orientation of the Hong Kong government therefore casts a long shadow over the future of our economy. With the rules of the game modified to accommodate more pro-Beijing and pro-business elements, some people foresee a return to a conservative and business-oriented agenda that upholds capitalism and ensures continued economic growth. This view is perhaps too optimistic (or pessimistic, depending on one's perspective). Despite his professed allegiance to the free market, the Chief Executive has made it clear that he is not averse to intervention on important issues affecting people's livelihood, thereby leaving much room for political manoeuvring and interference in the markets. Besides, the clock cannot be turned back, no matter how the political game is changed after 1997. Trying to banish politicians with grassroots support from the political establishment will only escalate social tension and confrontation. Nor is it so obvious that a business-dominated administration will safeguard free markets. Competition is for those who cannot monopolize; few firms will balk at abusing political power for economic rents if they can get away with it. This can be a particular problem in Hong Kong after 1997 due to the prevalence of political interference in economic activities in China. Repeated pledges by leaders of both Hong Kong and China to uphold the Basic Law will probably not stop business interests on both sides of the border from trying to seek favours when the stakes are high.

A return to the ways of the old days is therefore neither feasible nor desirable. What we need is a new political structure that can defend the market from political interference from within and without the Hong Kong Special Administrative Region, leaving economic decisions to the market. Better channels of communication must also be maintained among business, labour, and the government so that issues of potential conflict can be resolved through flexible and innovative solutions that do not impose too many constraints on market mechanisms. Active non-intervention may seem old fashioned, and the oft-repeated pledge of "One Country, Two Systems" might have become a cliché, but they still remain the most important micro and macro principles on which the economic success of the future Hong Kong rests.

Bibliography

1. Abraham, Katharine G. and Lawrence F. Katz (1996). "Cyclical Unemployment: Sectoral Shifts or Aggregate Disturbances?" *Journal of Political Economy* 94 (June): 507–522.

2. Altonji, Joseph G. and David Card (1991). "The Effect of Immigration on the Labor Market Outcomes of Less-Skilled Natives," *Immigration, Trade and the Labor Market,* eds. J. M. Abowd and R. B. Freeman. Chicago: University of Chicago Press.

3. Angrist, Joshua D. and Victor Lavy (1997). "The Effect of a Change in Language of Instruction on the Returns to Schooling in Morocco," *Journal of Labor Economy* 15 (January, Part 2): S48–S76.

4. Ashenfelter, Orley (1978). "Estimating the Effect of Training Programs on Earnings," *Review of Economics and Statistics* 61: 47–57.

5. _____ and David Card (1985). "Using the Longitudinal Structure of Earnings to Estimate the Effect of Training Programs," *Review of Economics and Statistics* 67: 648–661.

6. Barnow, Burt S. (1987). "The Impact of CETA Programs on Earnings: A Review of the Literature," *Journal of Human Resources* 22 (Spring): 157–193.

7. Barsby, Steve L. (1972). *Cost-Benefit Analysis and Manpower Programs.* Lexington: Lexington Books.

8. Bassi, Laurie J. (1984). "The Effect of CETA on the Postprogram Earnings of Participants," *Journal of Human Resources* 18: 540–556.

9. Bertola, Giuseppe (1990). "Job Security, Employment and Wages," *European Economic Review* 34 (June): 851–879.

10. Blau, Francine D. and Lawrence M. Kahn (1986). "International Differences in Male Wage Inequality: Institutions versus Market Forces." *Journal of Political Economy* 104 (August): 791–837.

11. Bloom, Howard S. (1990). *Back to Work : Testing Reemployment Services for Displaced Workers.* Kalamazoo: W. E. Upjohn Institute for Employment Research.

12. Bloom, Howard S. (1984). "Estimating the Effects of Job Training Programs, Using Longitudinal Data: Ashenfelter's Findings Reconsidered," *Journal of Human Resources* 19 (Fall): 544–556.

13. _____ and Jane Kulik (1986). "Evaluation of the Worker Adjustment Demonstration: Final Report." Bethesda: Abt Associates.

14. _____ and Maureen McLaughlin (1982). "CETA Training Programs: Do They Work for Adults?" Joint CBO-NCEP Report.

15. Borjas, George J. (1985). "Assimilation, Changes in Cohort Quality, and the Earnings of Immigrants," *Journal of labor Economy* 3 (October): 463–489.

16. _____ (1990). *Friends or Strangers: The Impact of Immigration on the U.S. Economy*. New York: Basic Books.

17. Carrington, William J. (1996). "The Alaskan Labor Market during the Pipeline Era," *Journal of Political Economy* 104 (February): 186–218.

18. Census and Statistics Department (1984). *Employment and Vacancies Statistics (Detailed Tables) 1984*. Hong Kong: Government Printer.

19. _____ (1992a). *Hong Kong Life Tables 1986–2011*. Hong Kong: Government Printer.

20. _____ (1992b). *Hong Kong Monthly Digest of Statistics, May 1992*. Hong Kong: Government Printer.

21. _____ (1993a). *Hong Kong — 25 Years' Development*. Hong Kong: Government Printer.

22. _____ (1993b). *Social Data Collected by the General Household Survey: Special Topics Report No. VIII*. Hong Kong: Government Printer.

23. _____ (1994). *Employment and Vacancies Statistics (Detailed Tables) 1994*. Hong Kong: Government Printer.

24. _____ (1996). *Hong Kong Annual Digest of Statistics, 1996 Edition*. Hong Kong: Government Printer.

25. _____ (1997). *Social Data Collected by the General Household Survey: Special Topics Report No. 14*. Hong Kong: Government Printer.

26. Chan, William (1996). "Intersectoral Mobility and Short-Run Labor Market Adjustments," *Journal of Labor Economy* 14 (July): 454–471.

27. Chau, L. C. (1988). "Labour and Labour Market," in *The Economic System of Hong Kong,* eds. H. C. Y. Ho and L. C. Chau. Hong Kong: Asian Research Service.

28. _____ (1993). "Labour and Employment," in *The Other Hong Kong Report 1993*, eds. Choi Po-king and Ho lok-sang. Hong Kong: Chinese University Press.

29. Chiswick, Barry R. (1978). "The Effect of Americanization on the Earnings of Foreign-born Men," *Journal of Political Economy* 86 (October): 897–921.

30. Dertouzos, James, Ellaine Holland, and Patricia Ebener (1988). "The Legal and Economic Consequences of Wrongful Termination." The RAND Institute for Civil Justice, R-3602-ICJ.

31. Dertouzos, James and Lynn Karoly (1993). "Employment Effects of Worker Protection: Evidence from the United States," in *Employment Security and Labor Market Behavior,* ed. C. F. Buechtemann. Ithaca: Institute of Labor Relations Press.

32. Dickinson, Katherine, Terry Johnson, and Richard West (1986). "An Analysis of the Impact of CETA on Participants' Earnings," *Journal of Human Resources* 21: 64–91.

33. *The Economist* (1995). "SCHOOLS BRIEF: One Lump or Two?" (25 November): 73–74.

34. Education and Manpower Branch (1994). *Manpower 2001 Revisited.* Hong Kong: Government Printer.

35. England, Joe (1989). *Industrial Relations and Law in Hong Kong*, 2nd. ed. Hong Kong: Oxford University Press.

36. Epstein, Richard A. (1984). "In Defence of the Contract at Will," *University of Chicago Law Review* 51 (Fall): 947–982.

37. Equal Opportunities Commission (1997). *Sex Discrimination Ordinance: Code of Practice on Employment.* Hong Kong: Equal Opportunities Commission.

38. Finifter, David H. (1987). "An Approach to Estimating Net Earnings Impact of Federally Subsidize Employment and Training Programs," *Evaluation Review* 11: 528–547.

39. Fraker, Thomas and Rebecca Maynard (1987). "The Adequacy of Comparison Group Designs with Employment-Related Programs," *Journal of Human Resources* 22: 194–227.

40. Geraci, Vincent (1984). "Short-Term Indicators of Job Training Program Effects on Long-Term Participant Earnings," Report prepared for U.S. Department of Labor under Contract no. 20-48-82-16.

41. Green, G., J. Coder, and P. Ryscavage (1992). "International Comparison of Earnings Inequality for Men in the 1980s," *Review of Income and Wealth* 38: 1–15.

42. Gueron, Judith M. and Edward Pauly (1991). *From Welfare to Work*. New York: Russell Sage Foundation.

43. Hamermesh, Daniel S. (1993). *Labor Demand*. Princeton: Princeton University Press.

44. Hayek, F. A. (1945). "The Use of Knowledge in Society," *American Economic Review* 35: 519–530.

45. Hirschman, Albert O. (1970). *Exit, Voice, and Loyalty*. Cambridge: Harvard University Press.

46. Hong Kong Government (1997). *Hong Kong 1997*. Hong Kong: Government Printer.

47. International Labour Office (1983). *Bulletin of Labour Statistics*, 1983–3. Geneva: International Labour Office.

48. _____ (1995). *1995 Yearbook of Labour Statistics*. Geneva: International Labour Office.

49. Juhn, Chinhui, Kevin M. Murphy, and Brooks Pierce (1993). "Wage Inequality and the Rise in Returns to Skill," *Journal of Political Economy* 101: 410–442.

50. Keynes, John Maynard (1964). *The General Theory of Employment, Interest, and Money*. New York: Harcourt Brace Jovanovich.

51. Kiefer, Nicholas M. (1979). "Population Heterogeneity and Inference from Panel Data on the Effects of Vocational Education," *Journal of Political Economy* 87 (October, Part 2): S213–S226.

52. Klein, Benjamin, Robert G. Crawford, and Armen A. Alchian (1978). "Vertical Integration, Appropriable Rents, and the Competitive Contracting Process," *Journal of Law and Economics* 21 (October): 297–326.

53. Kotlikoff, Laurence J. and Jagadeesh Gokhale (1992). "Estimating a Firm's Age-Productivity Profile Using the Present Value of Workers' Earnings," *Quarterly Journal of Economics* 107 (November): 1215–1242.

54. Labour Department (1993). *Report of the Commissioner for Labour 1992*. Hong Kong: Government Printer.

55. _____ (1996). *Report of the Commissioner for Labour 1995*. Hong Kong: Government Printer.

56. LaLonde, Robert J. (1992). "The Earnings Impact of U.S. Employment and Training Programs." Mimeo, University of Chicago.

57. _____ (1986). "Evaluating the Econometric Evaluations of Training Programs with Experimental Data," *American Economic Review* 76: 604–620.

58. _____ and Rebecca Maynard (1987). "How Precise Are the Evaluations of Employment and Training Programs: Evidence from a Field Experiment," *Evaluation Review* 11: 428–451.

59. LaLonde, Robert J. and Robert H. Topel (1991). "Labor Market Adjustments to Increased Immigration," in *Immigration, Trade and the Labor Market*, eds. J. M. Abowd and R. B. Freeman. Chicago: University of Chicago Press.

60. Lam, Kit-chun and Pak-wai Liu (1993). *Are Immigrants Assimilating Better Now than A Decade Ago?* Hong Kong: Hong Kong Institute of Asia-Pacific Studies.

61. Lazear, Edward P. (1990). "Job Security Provisions and Employment," *Quarterly Journal of Economics* 105 (August): 699–726.

62. _____ (1995). "Culture and Language," NBER Working Paper no. 5249.

63. Leigh, Duane E. (1990). *Does Training Work for Displaced Workers?* Kalamazoo: W. E. Upjohn Institute for Employment Research.

64. Lilien, David M. (1982). "Sectoral Shifts and Cyclical Unemployment," *Journal of Political Economy* 90 (August): 777–793.

65. Lui, Hon-Kwong, and Suen, Wing (1993). "The Narrowing Gender Gap in Hong Kong: 1976–1986," *Asian Economic Journal* 7 (July): 167–180.

66. _____ (1996). "Does School Quality Matter? Evidence from the Hong Kong Experience," Working paper (May).

67. Lui, Tai-Lok (1994). *Waged Work at Home*. Aldershot: Avebury.

68. MacLeod, W. Bentley and James M. Malcomson (1989). "Implicit Contracts, Incentive Compatibility, and Involuntary Unemployment," *Econometrica* 57 (March): 447–480.

69. McManus, Walter S., William Gould, and Finis Welch (1983). "Earnings of Hispanic Men: The Role of English Language Proficiency," *Journal of Labor Economy* 1 (April): 101–130.

70. Mincer, Jacob and Solomon Polachek (1974). "Family Investments in Human Capital Earnings for Women," *Journal of Political Economy* 82 (Supplement): S76–S110.

148   Bibliography

71. Muller, Thomas and Thomas J. Espenshade (1985). *The Fourth Wave.* Washington: Urban Institute.

72. Murphy, Kevin M. and Robert H. Topel (1987). "The Evolution of Unemployment in the United States, 1968–1985," *NBER Macroeconomics Annual* 2: 11–58.

73. Nickell, Stephen (1982). "The Determinants of Equilibrium Unemployment in Britain," *Economic Journal* 92 (September): 555–575.

74. _____ (1986). "Dynamic Models of Labour Demand," *Handbook of Labor Economics*, Vol. 1, eds. O. Ashenfelter and R. Layard. Amsterdam: North-Holland.

75. Orr, Larry, Howard Bloom, Stephen Bell, Fred Doolittle, Winston Lin, and George Cave (1996). *Does Training for the Disadvantaged Work?* Washington: The Urban Institute Press.

76. Pencavel, John (1986). "Labor Supply of Men: A Survey," *Handbook of Labor Economics*, Vol. 1, eds. O. Ashenfelter and R. Layard. Amsterdam: North-Holland.

77. Reidel, J. (1974). *The Industrialization of Hong Kong.* Tubingen: J. C. B. Mohr.

78. Rose, Nancy L. (1987). "Labor Rent Sharing and Regulation: Evidence from the Trucking Industry," *Journal of Political Economy* 95 (December): 1146–1178.

79. Simon, Julian L., Stephen Moore, and Richard Sullivan (1993). "The Effect of Immigration on Aggregate Native Unemployment: An Across-City Estimation," *Journal of Labor Research* 6 (February): 299–316.

80. Skeldon, Ronald (1995). "Emigration from Hong Kong, 1945–1994: The Demographic Lead-up to 1997," in *Emigration from Hong Kong*, ed. R. Skeldon. Hong Kong: Chinese University Press.

81. Stephan, Paula E. and Sharon G. Levin (1992). *Striking the Mother Lode in Science.* Oxford: Oxford University Press.

82. Stretton, Alan (1981). "Is the Hong Kong Labour Market Competitive? A Comment on Turner's Thesis," *Hong Kong Journal of Public Administration* 3 (June): 110–118.

83. Suen, Wing (1994). "Estimating the Effects of Immigration in One City." University of Hong Kong Discussion Paper No. 159 (April).

84. _____ (1995a). "Recent Labour Market Conditions in Hong Kong," *HKCER Letters*, No. 32 (May).

85. _____ (1995b). "Sectoral Shifts: Impact on Hong Kong Workers," *Journal of International Trade and Economic Development* 4 (July): 135–152.

86. _____ (1995c). "Gender Gap in Hong Kong: An Update," *Asian Economic Journal* 9 (November): 311–319.

87. _____ (1996). "Employment and Labour Earnings," in *The Hong Kong Economy in Transition*, eds. H. C. Y. Ho and L. C. Chau. Hong Kong: Asian Research Service.

88. _____ (1997). "Retirement Patterns in Hong Kong: A Censored Regression Analysis," *Journal of Population Economics* (Forthcoming).

89. Tsang, Shu-ki (1994). "The Economy," in *The Other Hong Kong Report 1994*, eds. Donald H. McMillan and Man Si-wai. Hong Kong: Chinese University Press.

90. Turner, H. A. (1980). *The Last Colony: But Whose?* Cambridge: Cambridge University Press.

91. _____, Patricia Fosh, and Sek Hong Ng (1991). *Between Two Societies: Hong Kong Labour in Transition*. Hong Kong: Centre of Asian Studies.

92. Westat (1981). "Summary of Net Impact Results," Report prepared for the U.S. Department of Labor under Contract No. 23-24-75-07.

93. Williams, Kevin (1990). *An Introduction to Hong Kong Employment Law*. Hong Kong: Oxford University Press.

94. Wong, Yue-Chim (1983). "Outworkers." University of Hong Kong Discussion Paper No. 25 (November).

Index

About the Authors

Wing Suen (PhD, Washington) is Senior Lecturer at the School of Economics and Finance, The University of Hong Kong. He graduated from the University of Washington in 1988. His main research interests are in microeconomics and labour economics. Recent publications cover such topics as the gender gap, the impact of sectoral shifts on Hong Kong, retirement patterns, wage inequality, and wage regressions.

William Chan (PhD, Chicago) has taught at The Chinese University of Hong Kong, and is currently Lecturer at the School of Economics and Finance, The University of Hong Kong. He is also a frequent visitor to the Hoover Institution at Stanford University. A labour economist, his interests are in the cyclical adjustment of labour markets, internal dynamics of firms, employees retraining, and mandatory retirement fund.

The Hong Kong Economic Policy Studies Series